Modern Critical Interpretations

Adventures of Huckleberry Finn

Animal Farm

Antony and Cleopatra

Beowulf

Billy Budd, Benito Cereno,
  Bartleby the Scrivener,
  and Other Tales

The Castle

The Crucible

Death of a Salesman

The Divine Comedy

Dubliners

Endgame

Exodus

A Farewell to Arms

Frankenstein

The General Prologue to the
  Canterbury Tales

The Glass Menagerie

The Gospels

The Grapes of Wrath

The Great Gatsby

Gulliver's Travels

Hamlet

Heart of Darkness

I Know Why the Caged Bird Sings

The Iliad

The Importance of Being Earnest

Invisible Man

Jane Eyre

Jude the Obscure

Julius Caesar

King Lear

Lord of the Flies

Macbeth

Major Barbara

The Metamorphosis

A Midsummer Night's Dream

Moby-Dick

Murder in the Cathedral

My Ántonia

Native Son

1984

The Odyssey

Oedipus Rex

The Old Man and the Sea

Othello

Paradise Lost

A Portrait of the Artist as a
  Young Man

Pride and Prejudice

The Rainbow

The Red Badge of Courage

The Red and the Black

The Scarlet Letter

The Sonnets

The Sound and the Fury

A Streetcar Named Desire

The Sun Also Rises

Their Eyes Were Watching God

A Tale of Two Cities

The Tales of Poe

The Tempest

Tess of the D'Urbervilles

To Kill a Mockingbird

Ulysses

Waiting for Godot

Walden

The Waste Land

Wuthering Heights

Modern Critical Interpretations

George Orwell's
ANIMAL FARM

Edited and with an introduction by
Harold Bloom
Sterling Professor of the Humanities
Yale University

CHELSEA HOUSE PUBLISHERS
Philadelphia

© 1999 by Chelsea House Publishers, a division of
Main Line Book Co.

Introduction © 1999 by Harold Bloom

Printed and bound in the United States of America

10 9 8 7 6 5 4 3 2

∞ The paper used in this publication meets the minimum
requirements of the American National Standard for
Permanence of Paper for Printed Library Materials,
Z39.48-1984

Library of Congress Cataloging-in-Publication Data

Animal Farm / edited and with an introduction by
Harold Bloom.
        p. 160   cm. — (Modern critical interpretations)
    Includes bibliographical references (p.) and index.
    ISBN 0-7910-4774-1
    1. Orwell, George, 1903-1950. Animal farm.
  2. Politics and literature—Great Britain—History—20th
century. 3. Political fiction, English—History and criticism.
4. Fables, English—History and criticism.   5. Animals in
literature.   I. Bloom,Harold.   II. Series.
PR6029.R8A722 1998
823'.912—dc21   98-15483
                                                    CIP

Contents

Editor's Note   vii

Introduction   1
  Harold Bloom

Orwell and Marxism   3
  Northrop Frye

Animal Farm   7
  Robert A. Lee

Animal Farm: The Burden of Consciousness   25
  Richard I. Smyer

The Making of *Animal Farm*   29
  Bernard Crick

Political Fiction and Patriarchal Fantasy   45
  Daphne Patai

The Utopian Shipwreck   61
  Patrick Reilly

Ant Farm: An Orwellian Allegory   91
  Robert Solomon

George Orwell's *Animal Farm*:
A Twentieth-Century Beast Fable   109
  Laraine Fergenson

Revolution on Animal Farm:
Orwell's Neglected Commentary   119
    V.C. Letemendia

Animal Farm Fifty Years On   131
    Michael Peters

Chronology   135

Contributors   139

Bibliography   141

Acknowledgments   143

Index   145

Editor's Note

This volume gathers together a representative selection of the most useful criticism available on George Orwell's satire, *Animal Farm*. My Introduction considers the involuntary relationship of *Animal Farm* to children's literature, and then amiably suggests how it could serve as a satire on current politically correct conformism in our institutions of higher education.

Northrop Frye's early review of *Animal Farm* begins the historical sequence of criticism by expressing reservations about how deeply searching Orwell's satire truly is.

Robert A. Lee emphasizes the theme of the corruption of language, while Richard I. Smyer centers upon how their mental incapacity preserves Orwell's animals from any consciousness of evil.

The process that brought *Animal Farm* into being is described by Bernard Crick, after which Daphne Patai, writing from a feminist perspective, condemns Orwell for "patriarchal fantasy."

Patrick Reilly stresses Orwell's satiric affinities to Swift, while Robert Solomon attempts an experiment of assimilating Orwell's allegory to an "Ant Farm."

The genre of beast fable in regard to *Animal Farm* is studied by Laraine Fergenson, after which V.C. Letemendia applies two neglected prefaces by Orwell to the task of commenting upon this fairy story for adults.

Michael Peters concludes this volume by considering the several ways in which Orwell reacted to the unexpected success of *Animal Farm*.

Introduction

*A*nimal Farm is a beast fable, more in the mode of Jonathan Swift's savage indignation than in Chaucer's gentler irony. George Orwell was startled when the book became children's literature, rather like *Gulliver's Travels* before it. And yet that is what saves the book aesthetically; *Nineteen Eighty-Four* is very thin when compared to *Animal Farm*. Boxer the cart-horse, Clover the mare, and Benjamin the donkey all have considerably more personality than does Winston Smith, the protagonist of *Nineteen Eighty-Four*. Fable necessarily suited Orwell better than the novel, because he was essentially an essayist and a satirist, and not a storyteller. *Animal Farm* is best regarded as a fusion of satirical political pamphlet and beast fable, but since the collapse of the Soviet Union, the historical aspect of the book necessarily has faded. The end of Stalinism removed the immediacy of *Animal Farm*, which now survives only by its pathos. Children are the book's best audience because of its simplicity and directness. Something in Orwell entertained a great nostalgia for an older, rural England, one that preceded industrial blight. The vision of Old Major, the boar who prophesies the transformation of Manor Farm into Animal Farm, is essentially Orwell's own ideal, and has a childlike quality that is very poignant.

It is very difficult to understand the psychology of any of the animals in Orwell's fantasy. How does Snowball (Trotsky) differ from Napoleon (Stalin) in his motivations? We cannot say; either Orwell does not know or he does not care. We are moved by poor Boxer, who works himself to death for the supposed common good, but we could not describe Boxer's personality. Even as a fabulist, Orwell has acute limitations; he could not create distincts. He was a considerable moralist, who passionately championed individuality, but he had no ability to translate that passion into imagining separate individuals. The creatures of Animal Farm compare poorly to those of Kenneth Grahame's *The Wind in the Willows*. Toad of Toad Hall and Badger are sustained literary characters; Boxer and Benjamin are not.

1

Whether *Animal Farm* truly can survive as children's literature seems to me rather doubtful, in the longest perspective.

Still, the narrative of *Animal Farm* is ingenious, and its twists retain a certain charm. The plain decency of Orwell's outlook still comes through clearly, and his fable's force is benign. Like his hero, the sublime Charles Dickens, Orwell was a "free intelligence," and his liberal passion against ideology is now his best legacy. Our era is again ideological, and *Animal Farm* now would make most sense if it satirized not the Soviet tyranny but the political correctness that blights our universities. Those resenters of individuality, for whom "social energies" are everything and personal genius is nothing, are now our Napoleons and Snowballs. Orwell's liberalism finds no home in Departments of Resentment. He should have lived to revise *Animal Farm* into a satire upon the way we teach now; and upon the way most fail to learn Orwell's longing for "free intelligence," which would find little to encourage it in English-speaking higher education as we approach the Millennium. Liberal humanism and individualist anarchism are condemned by our current gender-and-power dogmatists in the name of a new conformism. Its motto might well be: "All animals are resentful but some are more resentful than others."

NORTHROP FRYE

Orwell and Marxism

George Orwell's satire on Russian Communism, *Animal Farm*, has just appeared in America, but its fame has preceded it, and surely by now everyone has heard of the fable of the animals who revolted and set up a republic on the farm, how the pigs seized control and how, led by a dictatorial boar named Napoleon, they finally became human beings walking on two legs and carrying whips, just as the old Farmer Jones had done. At each stage of this receding revolution, one of the seven principles of the original rebellion becomes corrupted, so that "no animal shall kill any other animal" has added to it the words "without cause" when there is a great slaughter of the so-called sympathizers of an exiled pig named Snowball, and "no animal shall sleep in a bed" takes on "with sheets" when the pigs move into the human farmhouse and monopolize its luxuries. Eventually there is only one principle left, modified to "all animals are equal, but some are more equal than others," as Animal Farm, its name changed back to Manor Farm, is welcomed into the community of human farms again after its neighbors have realized that it makes its "lower" animals work harder on less food than any other farm, so that the model workers' republic becomes a model of exploited labor.

The story is very well written, especially the Snowball episode, which suggests that the Communist "Trotskyite" is a conception on much the same

From *Northrop Frye: On Culture and Literature: A Collection of Review Essays*. © 1978 by Northrop Frye.

mental plane as the Nazi "Jew," and the vicious irony of the end of Boxer the workhorse is perhaps really great satire. On the other hand, the satire on the episode corresponding to the German invasion seems to me both silly and heartless, and the final metamorphosis of pigs into humans is a fantastic disruption of the sober logic of the tale. The reason for the change in method was to conclude the story by showing the end of Communism under Stalin as a replica of its beginning under the Czar. Such an alignment is, of course, completely nonsense, and as Mr. Orwell must know it to be nonsense, his motive for adopting it was presumably that he did not know how otherwise to get his allegory rounded off with a neat, epigrammatic finish.

Animal Farm adopts one of the classical formulas of satire, the corruption of principle by expediency, of which Swift's *Tale of a Tub* is the greatest example. It is an account of the bogging down of Utopian aspirations in the quicksand of human nature which could have been written by a contemporary of Artemus Ward about one of the cooperative communities attempted in America during the last century. But for the same reason, it completely misses the point as satire on the Russian development of Marxism, and as expressing the disillusionment which many men of goodwill feel about Russia. The reason for that disillusionment would be much better expressed as the corruption of expediency by principle. For the whole point about Marxism was surely that it was the first revolutionary movement in history which attempted to start with a concrete historical situation instead of vast, a priori generalizations of the "all men are equal" type, and which aimed at scientific rather than Utopian objectives. Marx and Engels worked out a revolutionary technique based on an analysis of history known as dialectical materialism, which appeared in the nineteenth century at a time when metaphysical materialism was a fashionable creed, but which Marx and Engels always insisted was a quite different thing from metaphysical materialism.

Today, in the Western democracies, the Marxist approach to historical and economic problems is, whether he realizes it or not, an inseparable part of the modern educated man's consciousness, no less than electrons or dinosaurs, while metaphysical materialism is as dead as the dodo, or would be if it were not for one thing. For a number of reasons, chief among them the comprehensiveness of the demands made on a revolutionary by a revolutionary philosophy, the distinction just made failed utterly to establish itself in practice as it did in theory. Official Marxism today announces on page one that dialectical materialism is to be carefully distinguished from metaphysical materialism, and then insists from page two to the end that Marxism is nevertheless a complete materialist metaphysic of experience, with materialist answers to such questions as the existence of God, the origin of knowledge, and the meaning of culture. Thus, instead of including itself in the body of modern thought and giving a revolutionary dynamic to that body, Marxism has become a self-contained dogmatic system, and one so exclusive in its approach to the remainder of modern thought as to appear increasingly antiquated and sectarian. Yet this metaphysical materialism has no other basis than that of its original dialectic, its program of revolutionary action. The result is an absolutizing of expediency which makes expediency a principle in itself. From this springs the reckless intellectual dishonesty which it is so hard not to find in modern Communism, and which is naturally capable of rationalizing any form of action, however ruthless.

A really searching satire on Russian Communism, then, would be more deeply concerned with the underlying reasons for its transformation from a proletarian dictatorship into a kind of parody of the Catholic church. Mr. Orwell does not bother with motivation: he makes his Napoleon inscrutably ambitious and lets it go at that, and, as far as he is concerned, some old reactionary bromide like "you can't change human nature" is as good a moral as any other for his fable. But he, like Koestler, is an example of a large number of writers in the Western democracies who during the last fifteen years have done their level best to adopt the Russian interpretation of Marxism as their own world outlook and have failed. The last fifteen years have witnessed a startling decline in the prestige of Communist ideology in the arts, and some of the contemporary changes in taste which have resulted will be examined in future contributions to this column.

ROBERT A. LEE

Animal Farm

Life itself is essential assimilation, injury, violation of the foreign and the
weaker, suppression, hardness, the forcing of one's own forms upon something else, ingestion, and—at least in its mildest form—exploitation.
—Nietzsche

Egngland was at war by 1940, and the publication of fiction was curtailed.
Orwell had gone to work for the Far Eastern Service of the B.B.C. in 1941,
where he remained, working "hard" until early in 1945. However, these facts
do not fully explain the hiatus in Orwell's fiction from *Coming Up For Air* in
1939 to the publication of *Animal Farm* in 1945. During this period, Orwell
was writing a great deal; many of his most famous, his most important, and
his best essays appeared. "Inside the Whale" (1940), "The Art of Donald
McGill" (1942), "Looking Back on the Spanish War" (1943), and "Arthur
Koestler" (1944) all appeared in this period; Orwell's sociological and patri-
otic tract, *The Lion and the Unicorn: Socialism and the English Genius*, was
published in 1941. There appears to be a movement from novelist to essayist,
to that genre in which Orwell is considered by many to do his best work. We
do know, however, that during this period he was working diligently on
Animal Farm; it was, said Orwell, "the only one of my books I really sweated

From *Orwell's Fiction.* © 1969 by University of Notre Dame Press.

over." Yet the "sweating" itself could not have been protracted, for Christopher Hollis reports that it was "written between November 1943 and February 1944." A four-month period does not seem an especially lengthy period for a book which has been called a "masterpiece." Between 1933 and 1939 Orwell had published a book a year, and his relative inactivity following this period is not easily explained, even by the war.

In "Why I Write" (1947), Orwell remarked that "*Animal Farm* was the first book in which I tried, with full consciousness of what I was doing, to fuse political purpose and artistic purpose into one whole." Orwell's political purposes, though varied, had been consistently present to that point in his career; however, their infusion into his novels had been the obstacle he had to overcome to achieve fully realized and coherent art. The polemicist and essayist, concerned with political problems, causes, and effects, found the form of art difficult. And the struggle for appropriate form had become more crucial following Spain, as *Coming Up For Air* witnesses. For Orwell, politics had been a *sine qua non*; the common constituents of imaginative writing—character, image, narrative—were for him obstructions rather than guideposts. He is thinking of *Burmese Days*, for example, when he says that it is "invariably where I lacked a *political* purpose that I wrote lifeless books and was betrayed into purple passages, sentences without meaning, decorative adjectives and humbug generally." Yet we also know that Orwell's impulses were toward "artistic purpose." Furthermore, his intention in the last years of his life was purportedly "to make a complete break from his former polemical, propagandist, way of writing and to concentrate on the treatment of human relationships." Despite Hopkinson's notion of a "complete break"—obviously, given *Animal Farm* and *1984*, Orwell never denied politics completely—some purposes of the essayist never left him. But Orwell had come to realize that the stance of the polemicist, never long hidden even in his self-termed "naturalistic" novels, must be abandoned. And no form suited the abandonment of this role better than the beast fable: Not only was the narrator, the potential polemicist, gone, but the demands of the appropriate conventions provided an impersonality and distance which created art, not journalism.

That the beast fable was a natural choice for Orwell is borne out by John Wain. *Animal Farm* is

> . . . so remarkably similar in its tone, and in the balanced fairness of its judgments, to the critical essays as to be, almost, seen as one of them. It is, after all, a fable, and a fable is closer to criticism than to fiction in the full imaginative sense.

Yet this is surely not the whole truth. Imagination must be given a more important role than Wain is willing to ascribe to it; and the underlying requirements of this form seem to me to run exactly contrary to "balanced fairness," indeed one of the consistent aspects in Orwell's essay. The essential characteristic of the beast fable is irony: The form provides for the writer "the power to keep his reader conscious simultaneously of the human traits satirized and of the animals as animals." It demands of the reader a constant awareness of the double vision: Animal allegory prescribes two levels of perception which interact to purvey the irony in comparisons and contrasts. Orwell's essays are ironic only when they verge on fiction, as in the near-tales "A Hanging" and "Shooting an Elephant." In the kind of essays Wain has in mind, Orwell is honest and straightforward; the tone is that of the open, forthright speaker.

The use of this form provided an approach to art that Orwell clearly needed, one that differed from the conventional socially oriented novels he had been writing where he had fallen into pitfalls he now was recognizing. The need Orwell felt to criticize and attack social evils could now be subsumed into an artistic mode which by its very nature provided contrast and hence criticism. Paradoxically, the loss of a putative narrator and the gain of impersonalness that Orwell found in this form allow for a more intense criticism of social injustice and inequity than he had managed in his novels. The beast fable is in many ways the ideal form in which to articulate attack. The presence of beasts provides a readymade vehicle for the tenor of the hatred in this essentially metaphorical mode. The correlation of a man, or a class of men, as swine or sheep allows savage hatred on the subnarrative level and concurrently provides the coolness of impersonalness in the facade of the narrative. As I. A. Richards says of the properly functioning metaphor, the vehicle should not be "a mere embellishment of a tenor which is otherwise unchanged but the vehicle and tenor in co-operation give a meaning of more varied powers than can be ascribed to either."

Whatever Orwell gained artistically with *Animal Farm* was matched by the popular success the book enjoyed. It was the first of his books to achieve substantial commercial success, was a Book-of-the-Month Club selection in the United States, had a large sale, and was translated into many languages. Perhaps for the first time in his life, Orwell was moderately well off. The economic prosperity the book brought him was paralleled by critical accolades, and to this day *Animal Farm* is of all his works the most consistently praised. A judgment such as that of Frederick Karl, who finds the book a failure because of the "predictability" of the satire, is rare. The consensus of approval is represented by a spectrum of praise that ranges from Tom Hopkinson's pronouncements that not only is it "by far Orwell's finest book," but it is one of only two present-day books so good that before it "the critic abdicates," to Sir Richard Rees's only slightly less enthusiastic encomium that the book is a "little masterpiece" in form and style.

Because *Animal Farm* is so different from anything else that Orwell wrote, it is difficult to assess it in relation to his other works. It deserves much praise simply for succeeding despite the problems that this form and Orwell's particular use of it contain. I am thinking of the dangers of allegory in general and of the specific political allegory that informs *Animal Farm*. The principal danger of allegory in fiction is artificiality: The secondary level may demand such precise equivalents that it comes to dominate the tale, with the result that the primary narrative loses its pretense of reality and spontaneity. I think it is clear that this does not happen in *Animal Farm*. The allegory of the Russian Revolution and subsequent events is probably only noticeable to the eye which has been made aware of it.

Briefly, the narrative sets up equivalents with the history of political action in Russia from roughly 1917 to the Second World War. Major and Snowball are Lenin and Trotsky; Napoleon is Stalin; and the warring farms and farmers around Manor Farm naturally come to stand for Germany (Frederick) and the Allies (Pilkington). Certain events in the story are said to represent events of history: The timber deal, in which Frederick later reneges on the animals, is of course the short-lived Russo-German alliance of 1939; the card game at the end of the book is supposed to represent the Teheran Conference following the war. The correlations are more elaborate than this, and while there are some inconsistencies in the precise political allegory it is notable that one need pay little heed to this to understand the book in its full political significance. Instead of being just an allegory of twentieth-century Russian politics, *Animal Farm* is more meaningfully an anatomy of all political revolutions. As A. E. Dyson says, *Animal Farm* "is by no means about Russia alone. Orwell is concerned to show how revolutionary ideals of justice, equality and fraternity always shatter in the event." I would submit that the implications of this little book are wider yet: It is not merely that revolutions are self-destructive—Orwell also is painting a grim picture of the human condition in the political twentieth century, a time which he has come to believe marks the end of the very concepts of human freedom.

Nevertheless, the book starts with a relatively light tone. Mr. Jones— the commonplace name serves to diminish the importance of the human being in the story, yet gives a universal, "Everyman" quality—remembers to lock the henhouses for the night, but he is "too drunk to remember to shut the popholes." The picture of the drunken farmer, drinking his last glass of beer for the night and lurching up to bed while the animals come alive in the barn, reminds us of the cartoons (and Orwell's interest in the popular arts is surely at play here) and is primarily low keyed; at the same time, however, we note the irresponsibility of the farmer, neglecting—and endangering—those in his care. Later Jones will neglect to milk the cows, biologically a more serious omission; later yet, the pigs will also forget the milking, an ironic parallel that reveals the subsequent corruption of the revolution at the same time as it makes the pigs like humans—at that stage of the revolution a heinous sin. Nonetheless, the meeting of the animals while the humans sleep, though latently serious, forms a picture which is primarily whimsical. The description of the animals gathering for the meeting reveals the essential technique of the beast fable: Our concurrent awareness of both human and animal qualities and the several ironies which this perspective creates.

> The two cart-horses, Boxer and Clover, came in together, walking very slowly and setting down their vast hairy hoofs with great care lest there should be some small animal concealed in the straw. Clover was a stout motherly mare approaching middle life, who had never quite got her figure back after her fourth foal. Boxer was an enormous beast, nearly eighteen hands high, and as strong as any two ordinary horses put together. A white stripe down his nose gave him a somewhat stupid appearance, and in fact he was not of first-rate intelligence, but he was universally respected for his steadiness of character and tremendous powers of work. (p. 16)

The contrast between the strength of the horses and the fragility of the smaller, hidden animals places the scene unmistakably in the beast world; at the same time, the description of Clover's failure to get back her figure, a phrase Orwell surely chose for its commonplace, cliche quality, is representative of radical human nature. The menagerie, in fact, demonstrates a spectrum of human qualities and types, from the pigs, who take up the front seats in the audience, to Benjamin the donkey, the cynic of the farm, and to Mollie, the white mare, vain and foolish. These introductory descriptions are woven into the structure of the plot: For her vanity, Mollie will ultimately be excluded from the farm; in his cynicism, Benjamin will come to see but be incapable of changing the reality of the revolution; and the pigs will come to occupy not only the front but the total of the farm.

The awareness of simultaneous levels of animal and human existence is nicely maintained by Orwell in all the story's aspects. Major's speech, describing his dream in which man has disappeared from the earth and is replaced by animals, is at once a logical demonstration of wish fulfillment in the dream at a bestial level and a gospel of economic revolution easily understandable at the human level. ("Man is the only creature that consumes without producing" is, of course, an ironic variation of Marxian anticapitalism.) Orwell reinforces this irony by having Major's speech full of biological analogics: "The life of an animal is misery and slavery: that is the plain truth. But is this simply part of the order of nature? Is it because this land of ours is so poor that it cannot afford a decent life to those who dwell upon it?" We slide back and forth between reading this as Marxian dogma, excoriating capitalism and calling for a proletarian revolution, and reading it in terms of the mistreated animals—and we are reminded of the irresponsibility of Farmer Jones.

Moreover, there is the possibility of a fourth kind of irony: In his reading of *1984*, Irving Howe remarks that Emmanuel Goldstein's book, *The Theory and Practice of Oligarchical Collectivism*, imitates Trotsky's style in "his fondness for using scientific references in non-scientific contexts." Although there is a slightly different usage here, the employment of biological language in a political context is obviously related. We begin to be aware of the complexity of this seemingly simple little book. It is not simple political allegory, but neither is it merely classical satire built on multiple or receding planes." The various levels interact thematically: Animals are like humans; humans are, pejoratively, only like animals: human politics are really no more profound than natural biology.

The book is also constructed on a circular basis. Major's speech builds to the rhetorical climax of "All animals are comrades," which apothegm is immediately punctuated by the dogs' pursuit of some rats that they see. A vote is taken and the rats become "comrades," followed by the animals banding together against their common enemy, man, under the aegis of the motto, "All animals are equal" (p. 12). The remainder of the book will be a series of dramatic repudiations of these mottoes, a return to the tyranny and irresponsibility of the beginning. The only change will be in the identity of the masters, and, ironically, even that will be only partially changed.

At the opening of the second chapter Major dies, the prophet who articulated the revolutionary ideals and in whose name they will be carried out—and perverted. Snowball and Napoleon, two pigs, assume the leadership of the rebellion, aided by their public-relations man, Squealer. And these three codify the ideals of Major into Animalism, "a complete system of thought" (p. 18). But Animalism, obviously analogous to communism, is significantly instituted without any plan. The rebellion occurs spontaneously: Once again Jones neglects to feed the animals, who break into the barn for food when "they could stand it no longer" (p. 21). Jones and his hired man come in and the animals, "with one accord, though nothing of the kind had been planned beforehand," attack the men and chase them off the farm. "And so almost before they knew what was happening, the Rebellion had been successfully carried through: Jones was expelled, and the Manor Farm was theirs" (p. 23). Orwell stresses the spontaneity of the Rebellion to make clear that the social revolution per se is not the object of his satire. He emphasizes that no matter how bad things become for the animals later— and they do become bad—the animals "were far better off than they had been in the days of Jones" (p. 97). Though this fact will itself have to be qualified, there is a justness in the statement. Not only does the revolution's spontaneity diminish the importance of Napoleon and Snowball's plotting— and thus provide a dramatic irony about their supposed accomplishments— but the motive, hunger, justifies the revolution more basically and irrefutably than the soundest of political theories. The revolution sprung, not from theory, but from real, natural need. No matter how corrupt the ideals of the revolution become, Orwell never questions the validity of the uprising: The target here is not social—and socialistic—revolution, contrary to the many who simply want to see the book as a satire of communism, but rather the target is the inability of humans to live within a community of ideals.

The inevitable corruption of the revolution is presaged immediately. The animals have driven out their former masters.

> For the first few minutes the animals could hardly believe in their good fortune. Their first act was to gallop in a body right round the boundaries of the farm, as though to make quite sure that no human being was hiding anywhere upon it; then they raced back to the farm buildings to wipe out the last traces of Jones's hated reign. The harness-room at the end of the stables was broken open; the bits, the nose-rings, the dog-chains, the cruel knives with which Mr. Jones had been used to castrate the pigs and lambs, were all flung down the well. The reins, the halters, the blinkers, the degrading nosebags, were thrown on to the rubbish fire which was burning in the yard. So were the whips. All the animals capered with joy when they saw the whips going up in flames. (pp. 23–24)

The reaction is understandable; but the description of the inevitable and immediate violence that seems to follow all revolutions foreshadows that this revolution will suffer the common fate of its genre: reactionary cruelty, the search for the scapegoat, the perversion of the ideals of the revolution, and the counter-revolution. Thus, the good intentions of the animals are immediately endangered when it is learned that the pigs "had taught themselves to read and write from an old spelling book which had belonged to Mr. Jones's children." The pigs' reading ability is a valuable skill for the animals, one which is necessary to run a farm, even for animals. But it is also patently a human attribute, and one which already violates one of Major's cardinal tenets: "Remember also that in fighting against Man, we must not come to resemble him" (p. 12).

If seeds of destruction are immediately present, the positive aspects of the rebellion achieve their high peak with the codification of the "unalterable law by which all the animals on *Animal Farm* must live for ever after," the Seven Commandments.

1. Whatever goes upon two legs is an enemy.
2. Whatever goes upon four legs, or has wings, is a friend.
3. No animal shall wear clothes.
4. No animal shall sleep in a bed.
5. No animal shall drink alcohol.
6. No animal shall kill any other animal.
7. All animals are equal. (p. 28)

This "unalterable law" provides the major structural basis for the rest of the fable. From this point on the plot reveals a gradual alteration of these commandments, ending in the well-known contradiction that epitomizes the new nature of the farm at the end of the book. But here, Orwell's technique is of immediate irony: The animals are watching the commandments being painted on the barn when the cows begin to low, needing to be milked. They are milked, and the milk is placed in front of the animals, at which many "looked with considerable interest." But Napoleon, "placing himself in front of the buckets," will not even mix it with the hells' mash, as "Jones used sometimes to," and it disappears, eventually into Napoleon's own mash. Self-ishness is the note on which the chapter concludes, following the spontaneous and successful take-over of the farm and the articulation of unselfish ideals by which all the animals are to live.

The next concern on Animal Farm is to get the hay in, and we see further spoiling of the revolution's ideals as the pigs supervise rather than work. From the beginning, all animals are not equal. But one must be careful. In light of what is to happen, it is easy to see that the pigs' managerial role is further foreshadowing of the ultimate perversion of the seventh commandment, but this does not mean that the revolution is therefore wrong, or that Orwell thinks that all revolutions are inevitably self-corrupting. Both farms and revolutions need leaders, managers; and, for all their evil, the pigs are the most capable animals on the farm. Orwell may be suggesting—and this would be far more profound—that capable people are inevitably evil; or, conversely, that evil people are inevitably the most capable.

The capability of the pigs, and their management, is reflected in the success of the farm: There its no wastage, no stealing. It is the biggest harvest in the farm's history; in addition, though the animals work hard, there is no leisure. Each animal works "according to his capacity" (p. 32). The Marxian slogan at the base of the success of the farm seems to me to prove conclusively that Orwell does not question socialistic ideology. He does question the failure of ideology to accommodate human variety, implicit in the missing half of the quotation. At this point, Orwell specifically avoids mention of what goes to each animal: The irony of "need" is already apparent in what the pigs have taken and will be reinforced by the future miniscule gains of the other animals.

Orwell further stresses the human variability which undermines the best—or the worst—of systems in the character of Mollie, the vain mare more interested in ribbons than in harvests, and in the description of the cat, who disappears when there is work to be done. It is important that these animals are portrayed kindly and humorously: The cat, for example, "always made such excellent excuses, and purred so affectionately, that it was impossible not to believe in her good intentions" (p. 33). We soon learn the real nature of these "good intentions." The cat is spied one day talking to some sparrows who were "just out of her reach. She was telling them that all animals were now comrades and that any sparrow who chose could come and perch on her paw; but the sparrows kept their distance" (p. 35). We are reminded again of the natural, biological basis of the revolution—and remembering this we cannot blame the cat. If this attempt by the cat is at one level an ironic mirror of the pigs' later, horrifying "education" of the puppies into vicious trained killers, it is simultaneously natural—which the pigs' deed is not. Orwell reminds us of natural instinct and its inevitable conflict with political absolutism. It is to the point that Mollie soon leaves the farm. She is seen one day being stroked by a human on the outskirts of the farm; Clover finds sugar and several ribbons hidden under the straw in her stall. And so Mollie disappears, to be seen pulling a cart, her coat "newly clipped and she wore a scarlet ribbon around her forelock. She appeared to be enjoying herself, so the pigeons said" (p. 53). In political terms, she is, of course, a heretic, and her selfish behavior is inconsistent with selfless social ideals. But there is no intention on Orwell's part to criticize her. He rather suggests that too strict attention to the harsh, social demands of life obscures the love of beauty in the world. Any criticism seems rather to be directed at a political norm which makes the esthete the apostate.

For political and social demands do dominate life at Manor Farm; and the demands become more complex. Pilkington and Frederick spread stories about horrible conditions on the farm, stories which are contradicted by rumors among their animals about the wonderful paradise that exists on Animal Farm. Neither set of rumors is true, of course, and Orwell develops the consequences of such misrepresentation. The Farmers' animals begin to revolt in varying degrees—"bulls which had always been tractable suddenly turned savage, sheep broke down hedges and devoured the clover . . . ," while the humans, hearing in the song of Animal Farm "a prophecy of their future doom," invade the farm (pp. 44–45). It is not the social situations or conflicting ideologies that Orwell concerns himself with, but the misrepresentations, the falsification and distortion of fact, which he indicates leads ineluctably to disaster and misery. Falsification is at the heart of the main internal struggle on the farm, and the way fact is distorted and misrepresented is graphically pictured in the rivalry between Snowball and Napoleon over the construction of the windmill.

Snowball (who is a brilliant orator, compared with Napoleon, who was "better at canvassing support for himself in between times") conceives of a plan for a windmill, which Napoleon graphically disdains (he urinates on the plans). At the meeting in which the final vote for approval is to be taken, nine enormous dogs, "as ferocious as wolves," suddenly appear and chase Snowball off the farm; the dogs return and sit by Napoleon, wagging their tails, "as the other dogs had been used to do with Mr. Jones" (pp. 60–61). And it is just a short time until Squealer appears to announce blandly that Napoleon, "who had advocated it from the beginning," himself proposes the building of the windmill. More is suggested here than the simple power struggle attendant on all revolutions, or the more specific overthrow of Trotsky, the party theoretician and planner, by calculating Stalin. The symbol of the windmill suggests much about Orwell's complex attitudes toward the political concepts within the story well beyond the primary irony of the pigs' manipulation of the hopes of Animal Farm's animals. The windmill has Quixotic overtones: Orwell suggests that the way the animals focus all their efforts on building it is a false and deluded if heroic struggle. The windmill becomes the means by which Napoleon controls deviation; he uses it to direct the animals' attention away from the growing shortages and inadequacies on the farm, and the animals ignorantly concentrate all their efforts on building the windmill—but its symbolic nature suggests an empty concentration, a meaningless, unheroic effort, for the idea is literally misguided.

At the same time the symbol works in other directions. The windmill is analogous in the political allegory to the New Economic Policy. As such, it functions in much the same way as do other symbols of secular paradise in twentieth-century writing. Dams and bridges replace churches as representations of man's hopes for eternity; the windmill becomes a symbol of "secular heaven," placed in the future, but now in a temporal sense. I am reminded of Arthur Koestler's description of the Dnieper Dam, the "holy of holies," "a supernatural sight." This image and others accrue in Koestler's mind until he can quote a young Soviet official as "wonderfully" summing up the younger Soviet generation.

> We are believers. Not as you are. We do not believe either in God or in men. We manufacture gods and we transform men. We believe in Order. We will create a universe in our image, without weaknesses, a universe in which man, rid of the old rags of Christianity, will attain his cosmic grandeur, in the supreme culmination of the species.

While there is little doubt that Orwell was himself an atheist, I have reservations that he shared such a rhapsodic concept as the apotheosis of man to biological, social, and moral autotelicism. Organized religion and religious metaphors have been often used for varying purposes by Orwell prior to this book. Religious attitudes are thematically central to *A Clergyman's Daughter*: Religious metaphors are used for essentially ironic purposes in *Burmese Days*. In *Animal Farm*, precise religious satire is confined to Moses, the raven, who talks to the animals of "a mysterious country called Sugarcandy Mountain, to which all animals went when they died" (p. 20). Moses fled Manor Farm following the revolution, and when he returned later, he was "quite unchanged, still did no work, talked in the same strain as ever about Sugarcandy Mountain" (p. 128). The condemnation of religion is confined to its portrayal as an ineffectual force, with no real value, of no real harm. In *Animal Farm*, Orwell's secularism has no great need for the convenient metaphors that religion provides; the windmill is sufficient to suggest the hopeless transparency of the animals' goals.

The construction of the windmill, its subsequent destruction in a storm (during which the hens hear a gun go off in the background; the allusion is probably to World War I), and its rebuilding provide the linear movement of the plot in the rest of the book. The thematic development is centered on the progressive alteration of the Seven Commandments. Two monstrous indignities are suffered by the animals, but even these are thematically secondary. There is a bitter winter on the farm and rations become scarce: "starvation seemed to stare them in the face." A scapegoat is needed, and Snowball is conveniently used by Napoleon—who blatantly tells the other animals that not only is Snowball responsible for all the mysterious destruction that suddenly begins to occur on the farm, but that his brave actions in fighting the humans at the Battle of the Cowshed, *which all the animals witnessed*, had never happened. This is, of course, a direct prevision of the rewriting of history in *1984*. "Four days later," after being warned by Napoleon that Snowball's secret agents are still among them, the animals are ordered to assemble in the yard. Suddenly the dogs attack four of the other pigs and Boxer; but Boxer easily fights them off.

> Presently the tumult died down. The four pigs waited, trembling, with guilt written on every line of their countenances. Napoleon now called upon them to confess their crimes. They were the same four pigs as had protested when Napoleon abolished the Sunday Meetings. Without any further prompting they confessed that they had been secretly in touch with Snowball ever since his expulsion, that they had collaborated with him in destroying the windmill, and that they had entered into an agreement with him to hand over *Animal Farm* to Mr. Frederick. They added that Snowball had privately admitted to them that he had been Jones's secret agent for years past. When they had finished their confession, the dogs promptly tore their throats out, and in a terrible voice Napoleon demanded whether any other animal had anything to confess. (pp. 93–94)

In an obvious parallel to the purge trials of the 1930's, three hens come forward and admit to having heard Snowball speak to them "in a dream"; they are slaughtered. A goose confesses to pilfering six ears of corn, followed by a sheep who, "urged to do this" by Snowball, had urinated in the drinking pool, in turn followed by two more sheep who had murdered a ram. "And so the tale of confessions and executions went on, until there was a pile of corpses lying before Napoleon's feet and the air was heavy with the smell of blood, which had been unknown there since the expulsion of Jones" (p. 95).

Orwell has managed to dramatize, in two short, terror-laden pages, the very essence of this strange psycho-political phenomenon of our times: the ritualistic, honestly believed but obviously spurious confession. The ramifications of the motif in contemporary literature are many: One is reminded of a parallel such as Rubashov in *Darkness at Noon* and that, in a political age which denies individual selfhood, the only way of asserting one's self may be through pain or its extension, death. Ontologically and eschatologically, it may be preferable to die horribly and perhaps anonymously than to live as a cipher. However, I wish to consider the relative *insignificance* of the horrors that have passed, as physical terror becomes thematically subsidiary to the falsification of history and the denial of objective reality. Following this scene, the animals leave, led by Boxer and Clover. Boxer, unable to understand, thinks it "must be due to some fault in ourselves. The solution as I see it, is to work harder" (p. 96). And so he trots up to the windmill to resume dragging loads of stone to it. The other animals huddle about Clover on the hillside.

> It was a clear spring evening. The grass and the bursting hedges were gilded by the level rays of the sun. Never had the farm—and with a kind of surprise they remembered that it was their own farm, every inch of it their own property—appeared to the animals so desirable a place. (pp. 96–97)

Clover, looking down on this scene, remembers the promise and the hope of the revolution on the night she heard Major's speech, and her thoughts sum up the earlier images of the strong mare protecting the ducklings and recall the maxim at the base of the society, "Each working according to his capacity, the strong protecting the weak." Even here, she has "no thought of rebellion or disobedience," for the fundamental value of the revolution is reasserted: "Even as things were, they were far better off than they had been in the days of Jones" (p. 97). But the phrase "even as things were" implies too much, and so Clover, trying to somehow reestablish her continuity with that now quickly changing past, "feeling this to be in some way a substitute for the words she was unable to find," begins to sing the song, *Beasts of England*, which epitomized the egalitarian ideals Major expounded. The animals are singing the song when Squealer appears to announce that "by a special decree of Comrade Napoleon, *Beasts of England* had been abolished." Squealer tells the astonished animals that the reason is that "in *Beasts of England* we expressed our longing for a better society in days to come. But that society has now been established. Clearly this song had no longer any purpose" (p. 99).

The irony is of course the claim for a "better society," as the animals sit in the shadow of the heap of freshly slaughtered corpses. But the implications are more profound. Terror, bestiality, senseless death are all dreadful and shattering experiences; but they are at least comprehensible and do not radically alter the conceptualized values of the survivors. Far more terrifying is the overt alteration of consciousness which follows the slaughter, the blatant misrepresentation of the past, *which goes unchallenged*. The animals can only "sense" that the new song ("Animal Farm, Animal Farm/Never through me shalt thou come to harm") is different from *Beasts of England*. Squealer's pronouncement that the "better society" has now been established is uncontroverted. The commandments, which have begun to be altered recently, are now more rapidly and unquestioningly changed—and change pervades Animal Farm. A proposed timber deal vacillates between Pilkington and Frederick until the animals are forced to admit "a certain bewilderment, but Squealer was soon able to convince them that their memories had been at fault" (p. 107). Ironically, one of Major's prescriptions had been not to indulge in trade with the humans. Here the animals are not even sure whom the trade is with, much less can they remember past dogma.

The animals can no longer recognize reality, but they somehow manage to finish the windmill, concurrent with Napoleon's double-dealing with Pilkington and Frederick. We see the simultaneous strength and weakness, the goodness and corruption, that has evolved from the original rebellion. Despite all, the animals finish the windmill—they can accomplish a nearly impossible task—but at the same time, Napoleon, cheating and being cheated in his dealing, precipitates an attack upon the farm by Frederick and his followers (World War II, in the allegory). Though the animals win the battle, many are grievously injured and the windmill is destroyed. But Squealer declares that they have a "victory," "we have won back what we had before" (p. 116). And so the animals celebrate—each is given an apple, two ounces of corn for each bird, and three biscuits for each dog—while Napoleon gets drunk. The mere inequity, the surface irony is compounded by the inevitable falsification of fact. The next morning the animals discover that the fifth commandment did not read, as they had thought, "No animal shall drink alcohol," but instead "No animal shall drink alcohol *to excess.*"

It is not the threat of violence, even the radically inexplicable self-violence which the deracinated individual must, ironically, bring upon himself for his own secular salvation in a wholly political world, nor the war, nor the social injustice that man is suffering that is the cancer of our times, but the loss of "objective truth." Choices vanish in a society which has no bases for choice.

The most darkly pessimistic aspect of *Animal Farm* is that the animals are unable even to recognize their new oppression, much less combat it. The difference is that the pigs control language; Mr. Jones controlled only action—not thought. Orwell portrays at least three animals as being potentially able to stand up to the state (in an admittedly limited yet meaningful way), yet each is inadequate in a vital respect. Boxer has probably enough power and strength to overthrow Napoleon's regime. When Napoleon's vicious dogs attack him, Boxer simply "put out his great hoof, caught a dog in midair, and pinned him to the ground. The dog shrieked for mercy and the other two fled with their tails between their legs" (p. 93). But Boxer is stupid; he cannot comprehend the present, much less conceptualize the past. He ingenuously looks to Napoleon to see whether or not he should let the dog go;

when the slaughter is over, he retreats to work, thinking the fault must lie within the animals. Thus, his fate is not as pathetic, as some critics read the scene in which he is taken away, kicking in the truck, as it is the inevitable fate of utter stupidity. The most complex thought that Boxer can express is 'if Comrade Napoleon says it, it must be right," in the face of blatant, gross falsification. Boxer's basic goodness, social self-sacrifice, and impressive strength are simply inadequately used; the stupidity which wastes them suggests interesting qualifications about Orwell's reputed love of the common man, qualifications which become even stronger when considered in light of the descriptions of the proles in *1984*.

Clover is more intelligent and perceptive than is Boxer, but she has a corresponding lack of strength. Her "character" is primarily a function of her sex: Her instincts are maternal and pacifistic. She works hard, along with the other animals, but there is no picture of any special strength, as there is with Boxer. And even with a greater intelligence, her insights are partial. Things may indeed be better than they "had been in the days of Jones," but, in the context of the slaughter of the animals "it was not for this that she and all the other animals had hoped and toiled" (p. 98). Both perceptions are right, but both are incomplete. In both cases, Clover senses that there is something further to be understood, but just as Boxer uncomprehendingly moves to toil, so does Clover wistfully retreat to song—only to have this articulation of the past's ideals suddenly changed, without her dissent. A paradigm appears: Boxer is marked by great strength and great stupidity; Clover has less physical power but has a corresponding increase in awareness; the equation is completed with Benjamin, who sees and knows most—perhaps all—but is physically ineffectual and socially irresponsible.

Benjamin, the donkey, "was the oldest animal on the farm, and the worst tempered. He seldom talked, but when he did, it was usually to make some cynical remark . . ." (pp. 5–6). As archetypal cynic, Benjamin remains aloof and distant, refusing to meddle in the farm's affairs, but seeing all. He expresses no opinion about the rebellion; he works on Animal Farm "in the same slow, obstinate way" that he did on Manor Farm; he only remarks enigmatically that "Donkeys live a long time" (p. 33). Beneath the surface cynicism, he is, almost predictably, blessed with a heart of gold: He is devoted to Boxer, and it is he who discovers the plot to deliver Boxer to the glue-maker. But Benjamin is essentially selfish, representing a view of human nature that is apolitical, and thus he can hardly be the voice of Orwell within the book, as some readers hold. To Benjamin, the social and political situation is irrelevant: Human nature suffers and prospers in the same degree, no matter who is the master. He believes "that things never had been, nor ever could be much better or much worse—hunger, hardship, and disappointment being, so he said, the unalterable law of life" (pp. 143–144). We know too much about Orwell's social beliefs from other contexts to assume that Benjamin speaks for Orwell here. Yet, it is only fair to note that Benjamin sees most, knows most, is obviously the most intelligent and perceptive of all the animals on the farm, including the pigs. To a certain extent, he represents intelligence without the effectuating and necessary strength; perhaps more profoundly, he demonstrates the Orwellian heinous sin of irresponsible intelligence. The posture of assuming that only the very worst is inevitable in life, that change for the better is a delusion, and that the only alternative is a retreat into a social self-pity is exactly the posture from which Orwell presumptively jerks Gordon Comstock in *Keep the Aspidistra Flying*.

With the means of opposition to Napoleon's totalitarian rule so portrayed, there is little suspense in the outcome of the situation the novel describes. Years pass. Jones dies in an inebriates' home; Boxer and Snowball are forgotten by nearly all, for a new generation of animals has grown up. The situation on the farm is unchanged for most of the animals. The farm is more prosperous now, but the fruits of prosperity never pass beyond Napoleon and his comrades. And the attempt to judge whether the present situation is better or worse than it had been under Jones is fruitless.

> Sometimes the older ones among them racked their dim memories and tried to determine whether in the early days of the Rebellion, when Jones's expulsion was still recent, things had been better or worse than now. They could not remember. There was nothing with which they could compare their present lives: they had nothing to go upon except Squealer's lists of figures, which invariably demonstrated that everything was getting better and better. (p. 143)

Again, the condition itself is not as depressing as the loss of the rational criteria which allow evaluation. The denial of memory enables control of the present, and hence of the future.

"And yet the animals never gave up hope" (p. 144). For they do retain one ineradicable achievement: equality. "If they went hungry, it was not from feeding tyrannical human beings; if they worked hard, at least they worked for themselves. No creature among them went on two legs. No creature called any other 'Master.' All animals were equal" (p. 145). The social and economic hopes of the revolution may have become lost in the actualities of history, but the primary political gain of the revolution remains valid for the animals. Orwell articulates this one, final achievement of the animals. But within a page Squealer and Napoleon appear, walking on their hind legs. Yet even this sight is not the final violation of hope. Clover and Benjamin walk around to the barn to read the seventh commandment:

ALL ANIMALS ARE EQUAL
BUT SOME ANIMALS ARE MORE EQUAL THAN OTHERS (p. 148)

After this, "it did not seem strange" that the pigs take the humans' newspapers, that the pigs dress like humans, invite neighboring humans in to feast and drink, that the name of the farm is changed back to Manor Farm, and that, in the final image of the book, the pigs become indistinguishable from the humans. The book has come full circle, and things are back as they were. If this is so, Benjamin's judgment becomes valid: Things do remain the same, never much worse, never much better; "hunger, hardship, and disappointment" are indeed the "unalterable law of life."

Power inevitably corrupts the best of intentions, apparently no matter who possesses the power: At the end, all the representatives of the various ideologies are indistinguishable—they are all pigs, all pigs are humans. Communism is no better and no worse than capitalism or fascism; the ideals of socialism were long ago lost in Clover's uncomprehending gaze over the farm. Religion is merely a toy for the corrupters, neither offensive nor helpful to master or slave. But perhaps more distressing yet is the realization that everyone, the good and the bad, the deserving and the wicked, are not only contributors to the tyranny, are not only powerless before it, but are unable to understand it. Boxer thinks that whatever Napoleon says is right; Clover can only vaguely feel, and cannot communicate, that things are not exactly right; Benjamin thinks that it is in the nature of the world that things go wrong. The potential hope of the book is finally expressed only in terms of ignorance (Boxer), wistful inarticulateness (Clover), or the tired, cynical belief that things never change (Benjamin). The inhabitants of this world seem to deserve their fate.

One must finally ask, however, with all this despair and bleakness what are the actual bases for the tyranny of Animal Farm. Is the terrorism of the dogs the most crucial aspect? Is it this that rules the animals? Boxer's power is seen as superior to this violence and force. Is the basis of the tonal despair the pessimistic belief in the helplessness of the mass of the animals? Orwell elsewhere states again and again his faith in the common people. It seems to me that the basis of this society's evil is the inability of its inhabitants to ascertain truth and that this is demonstrated through the theme of the corruption of language. So long as the animals cannot remember the past, because it is continually altered, they have no control over the present and hence over the future. A society which cannot control its language is, says

Orwell, doomed to be oppressed in terms which deny it the very most elemental aspects of humanity: to live in a world which allows the revised form of the seventh commandment of Animal Farm is not merely to renounce the belief in the possibility of human equality, but in the blatant perversion of language, the very concept of objective reality is lost.

The mode by which the recognition of reality is denied is the corruption of language. When a society no longer maintains its language as a common basis by which value, idea, and fact are to be exchanged, those who control the means of communication have the most awful of powers—they literally can create the truth they choose. *Animal Farm*, then, seems to be in one respect only an extension of *Burmese Days*—the common problem is the failure of communication and its corollary, community. But if in *Burmese Days* their failure was contingent, in *Animal Farm* it is brought about by willful manipulation. The next logical step is seen in *1984*, where the consequences press to the premonition of apocalypse.

RICHARD I. SMYER

Animal Farm: *The Burden of Consciousness*

At one point in George Orwell's *Animal Farm* we are given a curious piece of misinformation. Ben the mule and the mare Clover are standing before the barn, on the wall of which is written the terrible truth about the revolution: ALL ANIMALS ARE EQUAL BUT SOME ANIMALS ARE MORE EQUAL THAN OTHERS. Because Clover's eyesight is failing, "for once," the narrator states, Ben consents "to break his rule" against reading. But this is not true. Once before he has broken his "rule" when reading aloud the sign on the side of the van which reveals Boxer's approaching death at the slaughterhouse (101).

An examination of Orwell's attitude toward contemporary affairs may help us appreciate the significance of this discrepancy. Pessimism, if not despair, is Orwell's dominant reaction to modern political events. Early in World War II he states: "I have known since about 1931 . . . that the future must be catastrophic." After the defeat of Germany, he foresees no likely alternative to either increasingly destructive wars or the rise of vast and enduring slave empires. Revolutionary activity has been not simply ineffective but positively harmful. "We are living in a nightmare," Orwell writes during the War, "precisely *because* we have tried to set up an earthly paradise." The Russian Revolution was inherently fated to degenerate into tyranny, with or without Stalin, for the idealism of all successful revolutions is "fatally mixed up" with

From *English Language Notes* 9:1. © 1971 by the Regents of the University of Colorado, Boulder.

the selfish longing to wield power. Attempts to reorganize society by force have only directed the course of history along a downward spiral—so that "once [a revolutionary] struggle is well over, there is always the [defeated] conservative who is more progressive than the radicals who have triumphed."

Characteristic of Orwell is the fact that his socio-political judgments constantly appear within the context of strong moral feelings. This is particularly evident in his assessments of the common people, the lower classes in general, whom he regards as the preservers of decency and humaneness. This reverence for the goodness of the lower orders, coupled with an equally strong conviction that twentieth-century politics is "a mass of lies, evasions, folly, hatred and schizophrenia," raises serious fears concerning the workers' involvement with revolutionary activity. Conditioned by his experience as an imperial policeman in Burma to regard even modest self-advancement as "spiritually ugly," Orwell, contrasting the "innate decency" of the working classes to the immoral opportunism of their leaders, is "almost driven" to the conclusion that "men are only decent when they are powerless."

As several critics have noted, the message of *Animal Farm* is that revolutions are bound to fail, merely replacing one group of oppressors with another. The ideals of equality and justice cannot be actualized because the existence of the liberated Farm demands a continuous interaction with the surrounding world of humanity which, in terms of the allegory, stands for oppression and exploitation. Paradoxically, the need to maintain an economically and politically viable society—a need which can be met only by reinstituting a hierarchical order and by trafficking with human beings—inevitably leads to the subversion of the beasts' utopian aims.

In Orwell's view (at least prior to *1984*), there is a great split between the outer world of political experience, of history, and the inner world of the spirit: "The vision of a world of free and equal human beings, living together in a state of brotherhood . . . never materializes, but the belief in it never seems to die out." It is not in the fallen world of historical reality but rather within the hearts of men that the purifying ideals of justice and equality can exist inviolate. Insulated from political reality, innocence is preserved; exposed to such an environment, innocence, perverted by power-hunger, is transformed into political villainy.

In *Animal Farm* the key factor in this transformation is intellectual superiority. "Generally recognised as being the cleverest of the animals," the pigs "naturally" become the teachers and organizers within the Farm community (13). It is important to note that because the pigs are the only animals able to substitute long-range planning for mere impulse, they are destined by nature to be the leaders of the revolution—a role which unavoidably exposes them to moral corruption.

Their loss of innocence starts during the second revolutionary stage (after the ouster of Farmer Jones) when, as a result of their expanded awareness, they begin developing an historical consciousness. As leaders, they must articulate goals and implement them by means of specific programs entailing institutionalized duties and restraints. In so doing, they are led to embrace the world of men, with its brutality and double-dealing. In effect, the development of political cunning—the end result of the pigs' intellectual capacity— involves an exodus from the innocence and stasis of the old Farm and a wandering in the spiritual wilderness of political activism, the unregenerate world of history. The Circe of awareness turns pigs into men.

For the humbler beasts, the failure of the revolution is closely linked to the fact that the Garden has not been lost. If they are still oppressed, they are also still untainted, still the communal embodiment of spontaneous brotherhood. Because their violent revolt against Jones springs from impulse and not from ideological formulations—"nothing of the kind had been planned beforehand" (16)—the beasts' animal innocence is not imperiled by power-hunger and the moral ambiguities associated with the assumption of a politico-historical identity.

Sheer mental incapacity preserves the animals from the consciousness of evil. Because their memories are short, the humbler animals cannot be sure whether or not they had earlier passed a resolution against trade; consequently, Napoleon's proposal to begin commercial relations with the outside world gives them only a "vague" discomfort (54). For the same reason, the animals need feel no anxiety about the breakdown of their social experiment after the pigs selfishly alter the wording of the commandment against sleeping in Jones's bed (57–58); and a slight rewording of the commandment against killing sets the naive beasts' minds at ease over the execution of supposedly disloyal comrades (76). It is a sign of the animals' relatively untainted consciousness—their ignorance of even the existence of political evil—that, as we learn toward the end, "Jones and all he stood for had almost faded out of their memories" (93).

Somewhere between the porcine world of cunning, immorality, and historical awareness, and the ahistorical animal world of impulse, innocence, and ignorance, stands Ben. Ben has a vague class identity: lacking the hominoid cunning of the pigs, he is not a leader; yet his mental capacity—he can "read as well as any pig" (28)—keeps him from being wholly within the animal realm. The circumstance that Ben, being a mule, is unique among domesticated animals in his inability to reproduce himself, identifies him with the educated middle class, which Orwell sometimes attacked for its lack of vitality. More specifically, Ben is representative of the intelligentsia. He is the modern intellectual who, unlike his mental inferiors, is cursed with the dispiriting awareness of the inevitable degeneration of revolutionary idealism. Figuratively as well as literally he can read the handwriting on the wall.

As already mentioned, twice—not once, as Orwell erroneously states— Ben has read, broken his rule. That is, more than once he has revealed his affinity with the porcine condition of intelligence and evil. To add to the ominous significance of the second transgression, the exercise of this homi- noid faculty involves the pronunciation of words which themselves represent the breaking of a rule—the subversion of the Seven Commandments estab- lished to keep the animals free from the corrupting effects of humanization. It seems, then, that Orwell, an intellectual acutely aware of his own threat- ened innocence in a world of political treachery, is too close to Ben to treat this figure with artistic objectivity. (It may not be too fanciful to identify the mule with Orwell, who never produced a child and who once expressed the fear that he was biologically sterile.) It is perhaps indicative of Orwell's help- lessness regarding the dilemma of the intellectual that, after reading the proclamation, Ben, one of the two surviving worker-animals who emerge as more or less distinct individuals, suddenly drops from the narrative. Unable to leave Ben within the thoughtlessly innocent realm of the humbler beasts yet morally repelled by the other alternative, Orwell can do no more than allow the mule to disappear into a limbo apart from either condition.

BERNARD CRICK

The Making of Animal Farm

In the same month as he joined *Tribune*, November 1943, Orwell began writing *Animal Farm* and he had finished by the end of February 1944. He knew that it would be a short book, for he wrote to Philip Rahv in December 1943, "I have got another book under way which I hope to finish in a few months." He was perfectly clear both what it was about (which could not always be said of his pre-war novels) and that it would cause trouble: "I am writing a little squib," he told Gleb Struve in February 1943, "which might amuse you when it comes out, but it is not so OK politically that I don't feel certain in advance that anyone will publish. Perhaps that gives you a hint of its subject." And in the very same letter he reverted to his interest in Zamyatin's *We*: "I am interested in that kind of book, and even keep making notes for one myself that may get written sooner or later." This is the first concrete evidence that he was planning *Nineteen Eighty-Four* even before he began to write *Animal Farm*. Some of these notes have survived.

The relationship between the two books is much closer than many critics have supposed. The form that each took was very different, but there was an intellectual continuity between the story of the revolution betrayed and the story of the betrayers, power-hungry in each case, perpetuating themselves in power for ever. And it was no boast on his part to say:

From *George Orwell: A Life*. © 1980 by Bernard Crick.

"*Animal Farm* was the first book in which I tried, with full consciousness of what I was doing, to fuse political purpose and artistic purpose into one whole." It was to become, its political message quite apart, sometimes indeed forgotten, the very model of good English prose almost everywhere English is learned; and even in the Soviet bloc it circulates in several widely read *samizdat* versions.

He explained the purpose and origins of the book in a preface he wrote in 1947 for a Ukrainian edition:

> . . . for the past ten years I have been convinced that the destruction of the Soviet myth was essential if we wanted a revival of the Socialist movement.
>
> On my return from Spain I thought of exposing the Soviet myth in a story that could be easily understood by almost anyone and which could be easily translated into other languages. However the actual details of the story did not come to me for some time until one day (I was then living in a small village) I saw a little boy, perhaps ten years old, driving a huge cart-horse along a narrow path, whipping it whenever it tried to turn. It struck me that if only such animals became aware of their strength we should have no power over them, and that men exploit animals in much the same way as the rich exploit the proletariat.
>
> I proceeded to analyze Marx's theory from the animal's point of view. . . .

Thus he reminded his readers, just as he was beginning to write *Nineteen Eighty-Four*, that *Animal Farm* had been "in my mind for a period of six years before it was actually written." He took pains to assert the political continuity and coherence of his writing after 1936 when he became both fervently Socialist and fervently anti-Communist. But he also warned his readers that though *Animal Farm* took various episodes from the Russian Revolution, the demands of the story came before literal history. The final scene of Jones and his men dining with the Pigs, for instance, was not meant to show reconciliation but discord. "I wrote it immediately after the Tehran Conference which everybody thought had established the best possible relations between the USSR and the West. I personally did not believe that such good relations would last long." The division of the world at Tehran and Yalta between superpowers who then fell out also underlies the plot of *Nineteen Eighty-Four*.

There was a peculiarity about the actual composition of *Animal Farm*

compared to that of Orwell's earlier books. He discussed it in considerable
detail with Eileen. She had been, she told her friends, always a bit disap-
pointed that he did not want her to read through and criticise his manuscripts before typing them out; only rarely, even back in Wallington days,
did he even ask her to type for him. After Eileen's death, he told Dorothy
Plowman that "she was particularly fond of and even helped in the planning of *Animal Farm*." He read his day's work to her in bed, the warmest
place in their desperately cold flat, discussed the next stage and actually
welcomed criticisms and suggestions, both of which she gave. Never before
had he discussed work in progress with anyone. Then the next morning
Lettice Cooper and Eileen's other women friends at the Ministry of Food
waited eagerly for a paraphrase of the latest episode. Eileen seemed excited
by it. And they shared not just her pleasure in the story, but also a mischie-
vous delight in speculating about the trouble that lay ahead for the reckless
author. Intelligent people did not miss the black comedy of Government
propaganda, particularly when it was Churchill's government, pumping out
plaudits to those "heroic Russian people" who so shortly before had been
"the dupes of the Bolsheviks in alliance with Hitler." Had not Churchill
himself said, the day after Hitler's invasion of Russia, that if Hitler were to
invade Hell he would pay a graceful tribute on the floor of the House of
Commons to the Devil? But for most people propaganda seemed to have
obliterated all bad memories of the Russian purges and the carving up of
Poland and the Baltic States with Hitler. That it was all *pour raison d'état* or
"for the emergency" seemed forgotten, even among some British Conservatives, let alone among the Left. Many English Conservatives of the old
breed never really took ideology seriously: politics was all a matter of
national self-interest, so Russia could be dealt with as Russia. To think of
Stalin as "Uncle Joe" might be going too far, but to keep on reminding
people that he was a totalitarian was as irrelevant as reminders of his crimes
were imprudent. But Orwell was not so much attacking sins of the past, still
less the conduct of a wartime ally; rather he was trying to clear men's minds
of cant and power worship so as to guard against what he feared would be
a future even more threatened by totalitarianism.

When the book was completed Orwell had no doubt of its merits. For
the first time he was fully pleased with what he had done. He also had no
doubt that he did not want Gollancz to publish it—though quite unfairly
he would include Gollancz in his future execrations against those who had
seen its worth but had not had the guts to publish it, or who had set themselves up as censors.

10a Mortimer Crescent,
London N.W.6
19.3.44

Dear Mr. Gollancz,
I have just finished a book and the typing will be completed in a
few days. You have the first refusal of my fiction books, and I
think this comes under the heading of fiction. It is a little fairy
story, about 30,000 words, with a political meaning. But I must
tell you that it is—I think—completely unacceptable politically
from your point of view (it is anti-Stalin). I don't know whether
in that case you will want to see it. If you do, of course I will send
it along, but the point is that I am not anxious, naturally, for the
MS to be hanging about too long. If you think that you would
like to have a look at it, in spite of its not being politically O. K.,
could you let either me or my agent (Christy & Moore) know?
Moore will have the MS. Otherwise, could you let me know that
you *don't* want to see it, so that I can take it elsewhere without
wasting time?

Yours sincerely,
Eric Blair

Gollancz replied to this provocative letter with understandable huffiness.

March 23rd 1944

Dear Mr. Blair,
Certainly I should like to see the manuscript.
    Frankly, I don't begin to understand you when you say "I
must tell you that it is—I think—completely unacceptable
politically from your point of view it is anti-Stalin:" I haven't
the faintest idea what "anti-Stalin" means. The Communists, as
I should have thought you were aware, regard me as violently
anti-Stalinist, because I was wholly and openly opposed to
Soviet foreign policy from the Nazi-Soviet pact until Russia
came into the war, because I have been highly critical of illib-
eral trends in Soviet internal policy, and because the last two
issues of the "Left News" have been very largely devoted to
uncompromising criticism of the Soviet proposals about East
Prussia, Pomerania and Silesia. Personally, I think it both

incorrect and unwise to label that anti-Stalinism; I call it the kind of criticism, whether of the Soviet Union or of any other State, that no socialist can renounce. There is, on the other hand, the anti-Stalinism of Hitler, Lord Haw-Haw, and the more reactionary Tories. With the latter, of course, I can have nothing whatever to do—and I should be surprised to learn that you can.

I suppose I ought rather to pat myself on the back that you apparently regard me as a Stalinist stooge, whereas I have been banned from the Soviet Embassy for three years as an "anti-Stalinist."

Yours sincerely,
Victor Gollancz

Orwell then sent it to him with a covering note asking for a speedy decision, reiterating that he did not think "that it is the kind of thing you would print" and saying that, naturally, he was "not criticising the Soviet regime from the Right, but in my experience the other kind of criticism gets one into even worse trouble."

Gollancz did give a commendably speedy decision.

Eric Blair Esq.,
10a Mortimer Crescent
London N.W.6

April 4th 1944

My Dear Blair,
You were right and I was wrong. I am so sorry. I have returned the manuscript to Moore.

Yours sincerely,
Dictated by Mr Gollancz,
but signed in his absence.

He said a little bit more to Orwell's agent.

Leonard P. Moore Esq
The Ride Annexe,
Duke's Wood Avenue
Gerrards Cross

April 4th 1944

My Dear Moore,
Here is the manuscript of *Animal Farm*, together with my note
to Blair. I am highly critical of many aspects of internal and
external Soviet policy: but I could not possibly publish (as Blair
anticipated) a general attack of this nature.

Yours sincerely
[Victor Gollancz]

Years later Gollancz maintained that Orwell was "a much over-rated writer."
This may have been sour-grapes, but it is plain that Gollancz turned down
the book as a matter of policy and principle. Even if he had had prophetic
powers of the book's incredible sales he would probably have made, though
with agony, the same decision. It was his own firm and he simply did not
want to publish such a thing.

So far, so good—from Orwell's point of view. But rage and alarm began
to mount, despite his anticipation of difficulties, at what happened when he
submitted the manuscript to Jonathan Cape. Cape's chief reader and literary
adviser, Daniel George (who also reviewed novels regularly for *Tribune*),
shrewd and experienced, gave it a fair wind, despite some uncertainty about
"its real purpose":

This is a kind of fable, entertaining in itself, and satirically enjoyable as a satire on the Soviets. The characters of Marx, Lenin,
Trotsky and Stalin can clearly be recognised, and incidents in
recent Russian politics are cleverly parodied. There is no doubt
that it would find many appreciative readers, though these might
not be of the class of which the author publicly approves, and its
real purpose is not made clear. Publication of it is a matter of
policy. I cannot myself see any serious objection to it.

Veronica Wedgwood, although about to leave Cape, also read it and was
strongly in favour of publication.

Jonathan Cape must have been eager to publish it for he wrote anxiously to Gollancz about the copyright position. Gollancz had Orwell under contract for his next three novels, and wished to hold him to that; so he told Moore and Cape that *Animal Farm* was both not a "novel" and was below the normal length for a novel (he had no interest in or rights over Orwell's non-fiction). Cape then began to discuss the terms of a contract with Moore, but also seeing it as "a matter of policy" thought it best to talk it over with a friend of his, "a senior official" in the Ministry of Information. The name of this official cannot, alas, be discovered. But to think it incredible that Cape sent the manuscript at all would be hindsight. The chronicler of his firm wrote: "It is not easy to recall now the force of moral rather than governmental pressure which deterred publishers from risking damage to the common war effort. . . ." The friend, in fact, followed up their conversation with a personal letter strongly imploring Cape not to publish a book that would so damage good relations with Russia. Cape was deeply upset and agonised over the decision, but fairly quickly, to the dismay and annoyance of Daniel George and Veronica Wedgwood, wrote to Moore as follows:

19 June 1944

My Dear Moore,

Since our conversation the other morning about George Orwell, I have considered the matter carefully and I have come to the conclusion that, unless the arrangement that exists whereby our author has to offer two works of fiction to another publisher can be waived, it would be unwise for us to enter into a contract for his future work. However, it does not seem to me unlikely that some compromise could be reached with Gollancz so far as this matter is concerned.

I mentioned the reaction that I had had from an important official in the Ministry of Information with regard to *Animal Farm*. I must confess that this expression of opinion has given me seriously to think. My reading of the manuscript gave me considerable personal enjoyment and satisfaction, but I can see now that it might be regarded as something which it was highly ill-advised to publish at the present time. If the fable were addressed generally to dictators and dictatorships at large then publication would be all right, but the fable does follow, as I see now, so completely the progress and development of the Russian Soviets and their two dictators, that it can apply only to Russia, to the exclusion of other dictatorships. Another thing: it would be less offensive if the predominant caste in the fable were not pigs. I think the choice of pigs as the ruling caste will no doubt give offence to many people, and particularly to anyone who is a bit touchy, as undoubtedly the Russians are. . . . I think it is best to send back to you the typescript of *Animal Farm* and let the matter lie on the table as far as we are concerned. . . .

> Yours sincerely,
> Jonathan Cape

Orwell was torn between rage and laughter at Cape's procedure. In the margin of a copy of the letter, where it suggested some other animal than pigs, Orwell wrote laconically "balls." (It is debatable whether the word "pig," offensive enough anywhere, is peculiarly offensive to Russians, but that is not the point. Cape had turned it down, not asked for innocent revisions.)

Something nearly came of it. Veronica Wedgwood was leaving to become Literary Editor of *Time and Tide* (a Liberal journal—in a very Right-wing sense). She asked the editor and proprietor, Lady Rhondda, a formidable lady, whether it would be possible to serialise the book. She was taken with the idea, even though it would have meant sacrificing almost all the literary pages for many weeks. But when Veronica Wedgwood took this proposal to Orwell, he expressed gratitude but said that the politics of *Time and Tide* were far too far to the Right for him, he felt it to be the wrong background for the book.

So Orwell then sent the manuscript to T. S. Eliot as a director of Faber & Faber.

> 10a Mortimer Crescent,
> NW6
> (Or "Tribune" CEN 2572)
> 28 June 1944

Dear Eliot,
This MS has been blitzed which accounts for my delay in delivering it and its slightly crumpled condition, but it is not damaged in any way.

I wonder if you could be kind enough to let me have Messrs Fabers' decision fairly soon. If they are interested in seeing more of my work, I could let you have the facts abt my existing contract with Gollancz, which is not an onerous one nor likely to last long.

If you read this MS yourself you will see its meaning which is not an acceptable one, at this moment, but I could not agree to make any alterations except a small one at the end which I intended making anyway. Cape or the MOI, I am not certain which from the wording of his letter, made the imbecile suggestion that some other animal than pigs might be made to represent the Bolsheviks. I could not of course make any change of that description.

Yours sincerely
Geo. Orwell

P.S. Could you have lunch with me one of the days when you are in town?

Even before Eliot replied, Orwell had made a hidden flick at Cape in a *Tribune* "As I Please" column of 7 July:

Nowadays this kind of veiled censorship even extends to books. The MOI does not, of course, dictate a party line or issue an *index expurgatorius*. It merely "advises." Publishers take manuscripts to the MOI and the MOI "suggests" that this or that is undesirable or premature, or "would serve no good purpose." And though there is no definite prohibition, no clear statement that this or that must not be printed, official policy is never flouted. Circus dogs jump when the trainer cracks his whip, but the really well-trained dog is the one that turns his somersault when there is no whip. And that is the state we have reached in this country, thanks to three hundred years of living together without a civil war.

Orwell's language was intemperate, but his description of what happened was all too accurate.

T. S. Eliot replied on 13 July.

I know that you wanted a quick decision about "Animal Farm" but the minimum is two directors' opinions, and that can't be done under a week. But for the importance of speed, I should have asked the Chairman to look at it as well. But the other director is in agreement with me on the main points. We agree that it is a distinguished piece of writing; that the fable is very skilfully handled, and that the narrative keeps one's interest on its own plane—and that is something very few authors have achieved since Gulliver.

On the other hand, we have no conviction (and I am sure none of the other directors would have) that this is the right point of view from which to criticise the political situation at the present time. It is certainly the duty of any publishing firm which pretends to other interests and motives than mere commercial prosperity, to publish books which go against the current of the moment; but in each instance that demands that at least one member of the firm should have the conviction that this is the thing that needs saying at the moment. I can't see any reason of prudence or caution to prevent anybody from publishing this book—if he believed in what it stands for.

Now I think my own dissatisfaction with this apologue is that the effect is simply one of negation. It ought to excite some sympathy with what the author wants, as well as sympathy with his objections to something: and the positive point of view, which I take to be generally Trotskyite, is not convincing. I think you split your vote, without getting any compensating strong adhesion from either party—i.e. those who criticise Russian tendencies from the point of view of a purer communism, and those who, from a wry different point of view, are alarmed about the future of small nations. And after all, your pigs are far more intelligent than the other animals, and therefore the best qualified to run the farm—in fact, there couldn't have been an Animal Farm at all without them: so that what was needed (someone might argue) was not more communism but more public-spirited pigs.

I am very sorry because whoever publishes this will naturally have the opportunity of publishing your future work: and I have a regard for your work, because it is good writing of fundamental integrity. . . .

Orwell bore Eliot no personal ill will for this. They corresponded on routine editorial matters without rancour later in the year. Yet the letter was in some ways a very strange one. Eliot offered such a variety of arguments, not all consistent with each other, to the same conclusion, but at least he took the book very seriously, which must have disarmed Orwell's personal anger. Plainly he says, in his complicated Eliot-like way, that "it is not our kind of book" and that further, whatever its literary merits, a polemical political book needs some positive conviction behind it from the firm. It would have been as odd for Faber & Faber to publish a revolutionary tract as for Victor Gollancz, at that time even, to publish an anti-Russian conservative one. The Trotskyite attribution is neither unfair nor entirely unexpected from Geoffrey Faber and T. S. Eliot's standpoint, and it is a more accurate reading than that it was to receive from some future Cold War warriors across the Atlantic (including his future main American publishers). The insistence on the inevitability of élites, however, that pigs are with us always, so preferably "public-spirited" pigs, is extraordinarily narrowing for any satirist, especially one capable of "good writing of fundamental integrity"; and the point about the integrity of small nations, precisely one of Orwell's own concerns, is either a sad misreading or a bad red-herring. The favourable comparison with Swift's skill and with *Gulliver* itself (how right Eliot was, how specific is the influence of the Yahoos and the Houyhnhnms on Orwell's fable) should surely have settled the matter, if literary merit was the touchstone. Swift too could have been viewed as untimely, imprudent and essentially negative. Eliot was lucky that Orwell never wrote a parody Eliot letter of rejection to Swift.

The touchstone, however, was not purely literary: Orwell had encountered a "political writer" almost as complicated as himself. If, that is, the letter of rejection is necessarily to be taken as Eliot's views in all respects: it could be a composite of several people's views. He was, after all, a partner of Faber & Faber, but Geoffrey Faber was the owner and took the financial risks. Eliot was punctilious and precise in never recommending publication, only commenting on a book's merits. Geoffrey Faber made the hard decisions, but he did not like writing difficult letters of rejection, such disagreeable tasks he often left to the loyal Eliot. What exactly happened in this case is obscure, but it is a simplification to say that "T. S. Eliot" turned down *Animal Farm*. It was rejected by the firm, a different and not wholly consistent animal.

Four days after Eliot's letter arrived, Orwell told Moore that "Warburg again says he wants to see it and would publish it if he can see his way to getting the paper, but that is a big 'if'." If that falls through, he said, he was not "going to tout it round further publishers . . . but shall publish it myself as a pamphlet at 2s. I have already half-arranged to do so and have got the necessary financial backing." Why did he not take it to Warburg in the first place, a publisher who had already handled two of his books? The answer must lie in Orwell's confidence in the merit of the book and his desire to see it published by one of the two best publishing houses in England. Years before, with far less justifiable confidence, he had sent Faber and then Cape the first and the rejected versions of *Down and Out in Paris and London*. He wanted that kind of recognition, at least for this book. Secker & Warburg, before their faith in Thomas Mann, Franz Kafka and Orwell had paid off, looked a very different house—small, lively but precarious and still nick-named, however unfairly, because of their courage and persistence in bringing out difficult Left-wing books, "the Trotskyite publisher." Political though the fable was, Orwell thought its literary merits should carry it to a wider readership.

It is odd that he lost heart too soon. Perhaps he was shocked that his new reputation did not prevent such a sudden return to the problems of how to get published at all that he had suffered in his youth. To be turned down by two great publishing houses, and to be as yet unwilling even to show the manuscript to Fred Warburg, seemed an inadequate reason for desperate measures like publishing it himself. Perhaps he felt that if the two most distinguished houses had not recognised its merit he would show the lot of them, he would eat worms and do it himself in thoroughly radical fashion. And he may have been affected by American rejections too. At some stage that year it was sent to the Dial Press who returned it, according to Orwell, with the comment that "it was impossible to sell animal stories in the U.S.A." It is possible, of course, that he believed that the hand of the M.O.I., once alerted, would reach everywhere; and also that he believed the rumours, as his excitable *Tribune* friends did, that Victor Gollancz was on the phone warning London publishers that this time that man had gone too far and was damaging the national interest.

Orwell may not have intended literally to publish it himself, although he approached David Astor, with much diffidence, for a loan of £200. Astor was willing but thought the project hare-brained: he counselled him to have patience with real publishers. But Orwell may have wanted the money more as a subsidy, for he next offered it to anarchist friends. George Woodcock was a member of the board of the Freedom Press, managed by Vernon Richards and Marie Louise Berneri; and he remembers sounding them out. She objected to it strongly, so it is doubtful it was ever formally submitted. Vernon Richards is adamant that it was never submitted, but he was in prison at the relevant time and might not have been told. Probably one or other of them advised Orwell that it would stand a chance if formally submitted, for the board contained many belligerent pacifists who knew his early wartime writings and attacks on them as pacifists only too well. Whatever their common hatred of Stalinism, of all "oligarchic collectivism" and their common ground with Orwell that there had been a revolution but it had been betrayed, they had not liked being called "objectively Fascist" in rela-tion to the war effort. They had neither forgiven nor forgotten. Their feel-ings are understandable. However, associated with them was Paul Potts who published and sold poems in pubs on broadsheets, mainly his own. (This enterprise grew, for a while, into a pleasant little imprint, the Whitman Press.) In a perceptive, if idiosyncratic, chapter on Orwell called "Don Quixote on a Bicycle" in his *Dante Called You Beatrice* (1960), Potts claims:

> At one point I became the publisher of *Animal Farm*—which only means that we were going to bring it out ourselves. Orwell was going to pay the printer, using the paper quota to which the Whitman Press was entitled. . . . We had actually started to do so. I had been down to Bedford with the manuscript to see the printer twice. The birthplace of John Bunyan seemed a happy omen. Orwell had never spoken about the contents. I had not liked to ask as any questions might appear to have an editorial accent. He had, however, talked about adding a preface to it on the freedom of the Press. . . . That essay on the freedom of the Press was not needed as Secker and Warburg, at the last minute, accepted the book.

The sentimental prose of *Dante Called You Beatrice* raises some of the same problems as Jacintha Buddicom's writing about Orwell's early years: the style has been taken as grounds for doubting the memories and judgments. Mr. Potts' book has its moments when fact and fiction blend rather uneasily and the chronology is a bit wobbly; but he knew Orwell well and he is a valuable and important source. The essential truth of Potts' account is shown by his being the only person who had ever heard of or who could remember "The Freedom of the Press"—a fiery preface to *Animal Farm* which Orwell did in fact write as a blast against self-censorship, but fortunately did not use. It was lost until 1971. People either did not believe Potts or did not notice his claim that there was a lost major essay (reviewers often have to work at such speed).

In the end the much-handled, dog-eared manuscript was sent to Fred Warburg late in July. The dramatic account Warburg gives in *All Authors Are Equal* of it coming to him out of the blue, of Orwell turning up during his lunch one day and dumping the manuscript on him with an urgent explanation of its contents, is contradicted by Orwell's letter to Moore in the previous month (already quoted), in which he says that Warburg knew about it, had not seen it but wanted to publish it. Probably Orwell came to him, rather shamefacedly, as a last resort. But Orwell's letter raises a problem. However enthusiastic Warburg may have been about Orwell, it is unlikely that he would have taken anything sight unseen. He had already, not surprisingly, turned down Orwell's "War-time Diary." Perhaps Orwell was merely making excuses to Moore for not wanting to send it directly to Warburg, as would have seemed to Moore to be less trouble, more sensible and even proper, from the start. Warburg is, however, amusingly frank about his hesitations once he had read it. Its merits were obvious, but so were the dangers of being its publisher in wartime. Warburg in his autobiography does not crow over Cape or Faber. He saw the dilemma very much in their terms but, despite some strong opposition to accepting the book within his firm, decided to run the risk. Under the rationing system, however, he was desperately short of paper, as he had already warned the suspicious Orwell.

The book was over a year in production and it was not published until August 1945, which was a very long time in those days, especially for such a short book. Orwell wrote to a provincial Labour journalist, Frank Barber, on 3 September 1945, "I have been surprised by the friendly reception *Animal Farm* has had, after lying in type for about a year because the publisher dared not bring it out till the war was over." And on 19 August he had written in a letter to Herbert Read that he had stopped writing for *Tribune* while away in France "and didn't start again because Bevan was terrified there might be a row over *Animal Farm* which might have been embarrassing if the book had come out before the election, as it was at first intended to." These two statements must be taken with a large pinch of salt in the absence of other evidence. It had not been "lying in type for about a year," for Orwell wrote in a letter to T. S. Eliot on 5 September 1944: "Warburg is going to do that book you saw but he probably can't get it out until early next year because of paper." Letters between Orwell and his literary agent show that complications about signing the actual contract also dragged on into March 1945. Orwell may well have been laying it on a bit thick about the delay after the difficult experience he had had in getting his masterpiece accepted at all.

For a moment George Orwell seemed to relapse into being Gordon Comstock again and lashed out in all directions. His feeling of being persecuted for plain speaking was heightened by the rejection in March of a review he wrote for *The Manchester Evening News* of Harold Laski's *Faith, Reason and Civilization*. He had agreed with Laski that the Soviet Union, for all its faults, was the "real dynamo of the Socialist movement," but he had criticised him for closing his eyes to "purges, liquidations, the dictatorship of a minority, suppression of criticism and so forth." The editor felt that this was against the national interest. Dwight Macdonald got to hear about it in New York and wrote an editorial in his *Politics* warning "how seriously the feats of the Red army have misled English public opinion about Russia."

So Orwell's harsh and bitter comment in the last paragraph of the unused preface is understandable, given the provocation and the circumstances.

I know that the English intelligentsia have plenty of reason for their timidity and dishonesty, indeed I know by heart the arguments by which they justify themselves. But at least let us have no more nonsense about defending liberty against Fascism. If liberty means anything at all it means the right to tell people what they do not want to hear. The common people still vaguely subscribe to that doctrine and act on it. In our country . . . it is the liberals who fear liberty and the intellectuals who want to do dirt on the intellect; it is to draw attention to that fact that I have written this preface.

DAPHNE PATAI

Political Fiction and Patriarchal Fantasy

In his essay "Marrakech," Orwell elaborates on the perception that came to him, during his stay in Morocco, that "All people who work with their hands are partly invisible." Describing the file of "very old women," each bent beneath a load of firewood, who passed by his house every afternoon for several weeks, he comments: "I cannot truly say that I had seen them. Firewood was passing—that was how I saw it" (CEJL, 1:391). One day he happened to be walking behind the firewood and finally noticed "the human being underneath it"—a woman. By contrast, he writes, his awareness of the mistreatment of animals was immediate: "I had not been five minutes on Moroccan soil before I noticed the overloading of the donkeys and was infuriated by it." Orwell then describes the small Moroccan donkey, a faithful and willing worker, in the anthropomorphic terms he was later to use for Boxer, the immense and hardworking cart horse in *Animal Farm*, and concludes: "After a dozen years of devoted work, it suddenly drops dead, whereupon its master tips it into the ditch and the village dogs have torn its guts out before it is cold" (1:392). In a fascinating example of his tendency to generalize from personal reactions, Orwell states: "This kind of thing makes one's blood boil, whereas—on the whole—the plight of the human beings does not. I am not commenting, merely pointing to a fact. People with brown skins are next door to invisible. Anyone can be sorry for the donkey

From *The Orwell Mystique: A Study in Male Ideology.* © 1984 by Daphne Patai.

with its galled back, but it is generally owing to some kind of accident if one even notices the old woman under her load of sticks" (1:392). The woman, Orwell had earlier explained, "accepted her status as an old woman, that is to say as a beast of burden" (1:391). Rebellion is not a possibility for her, any more than for the Negro soldiers (very visible to Orwell, however) described later in the same essay as unaware of their potential power (see chapter 4).

Orwell explained the genesis of *Animal Farm* in a 1947 preface to the Ukrainian edition of the book. For a decade he had "been convinced that the destruction of the Soviet myth was essential if we wanted a revival of the Socialist movement."

> On my return from Spain I thought of exposing the Soviet myth in a story that could be easily understood by almost anyone and which could be easily translated into other languages. However the actual details of the story did not come to me for some time until one day (I was then living in a small village) I saw a little boy, perhaps ten years old, driving a huge cart-horse along a narrow path, whipping it whenever it tried to turn. It struck me that if only such animals became aware of their strength we should have no power over them, and that men exploit animals in much the same way as the rich exploit the proletariat.
>
> I proceeded to analyse Marx's theory from the animals' point of view. To them it was clear that the concept of a class struggle between humans was pure illusion, since whenever it was necessary to exploit animals, all humans united against them: the true struggle is between animals and humans. From this point of departure, it was not difficult to elaborate the story. [CEJL, 3:405–6]

In Morocco, Orwell perceived the cruel labor of donkeys more readily than that of brown-skinned women. Though he abstracts himself from his description and attributes his reaction to all people ("merely pointing to a fact"), this is a characteristic perception for Orwell. We see it duplicated in his account of how he came to write *Animal Farm*. For when Orwell was ready to think in terms of exploitation that transcends economic class, he blindly leaped from class to species without pausing to consider the question of gender. It was apparently easier for Orwell to identify with the animal kingdom, exploited at the hands of "humans," than to note that buried in class and race divisions in the human world lay the issue of gender oppression.

The animals' perspective adopted by Orwell as the starting point for his fable leads him to a conclusion—that the class struggle among humans is "pure illusion"—which is itself an illusion. Although humans have been united in their exploitation of animals, this does not mean that they are united in all other respects. There can exist both a class struggle and a general exploitation of animals. Only this gross simplification, however, enabled Orwell to write *Animal Farm*; in fact, the choice of allegory allowed Orwell to turn his penchant for generalization, one of his fundamental weaknesses as a writer, into a strength, for, as Gay Clifford points out, "allegory invites its readers . . . to see the particular narrative as being also a series of generalized statements, and demands that concepts be identified simultaneously in their fictional and ideological roles." Clifford goes on to state that both *Animal Farm* and *Nineteen Eighty-Four*, like other modern allegories, "require a single act of translation (fiction to history for example) and then can be read as straight narratives whose moral significance is obvious. Indeed, without that clearly delimited act of translation they lose half their force."

Allegory, like myth, presupposes an audience that will respond in certain ways. This is one reason, Northrop Frye has observed, that critics dislike allegory, for it restricts the freedom of their commentary by prescribing its direction. In Clifford's words: "The idea that there are as many ways of reading a work of literature as there are readers is anathema to allegory." This observation is borne out by Orwell's anxious concern that *Animal Farm* be read "correctly." After the manuscript's rejection by Dial Press in New York in 1944, on the grounds that "it was impossible to sell animal stories in the USA," Orwell was "not sure whether one can count on the American public grasping what it is about," as he explained in a letter to his agent (CEJL, 4:110); and he even suggested that "it might be worth indicating on the dust-jacket of the American edition what the book is about" (4:111). Orwell need not have worried. When published in the United States in 1946, *Animal Farm* was the Book-of-the-Month Club main selection, and an unprecedented special letter was sent by the club's president to its members urging them to choose *Animal Farm* rather than an alternative title. It sold over half a million copies (4:519) in the club edition alone. Far from not being understood, it was immediately put to work as an anti-Communist text and to this day is taught in American schools, apparently for this purpose.

Patriarch Pigs, Maternal Mares, and other Animals

The psychological appeal of the animal fable is easy to understand: By projecting human conflicts onto animal characters, readers can avoid feeling threatened or overwhelmed by the real-world problems they encounter in this simplified and in many respects charming form. Neither the author nor the readers, however, are magically freed from their own prejudices by this displacement. On the contrary, a fable such as *Animal Farm* relies considerably upon engaging the reader's preconceived ideas. The author's particular concerns can be more clearly set in relief against a background of familiar and nonchallenging elements. In his fable, Orwell evokes not only our sympathy for certain animals but also our possible distaste for pigs, fear of barking and biting dogs, and awe at the size and strength of horses. But even in the early stages of his story he does not merely portray the animals as united in their animalness against the species *Homo sapiens*; nor, as the story develops, does he simply elicit "anti" feelings for the pigs and "pro" feelings for the other animals without further distinctions.

To be effective, an animal fable must maintain a delicate balance between the evocation of the animals' human characteristics and their recognizable animal traits. The reader must use both perspectives, the human and the animal, simultaneously, if the allegory is not to become ludicrous. Orwell provides a poignantly humorous example of this in describing how the animals went through the farmhouse after the revolution: "Some hams hanging in the kitchen were taken out for burial" (22). Even Snowball's writing down of the Seven Commandments of Animalism is endearing: "It was very neatly written, and except that 'friend' was written 'freind' and one of the 'S's' was the wrong way round, the spelling was correct all the way through" (23). Descriptions such as this occur at many points in the text, and their emotional appeal clearly comes from the childlike quality of the details. At this stage of the proceedings the reader sees nothing sinister in the pigs' newfound literacy. Again and again Orwell attributes childlike tastes and habits to the animals, their love of singing their anthem, "Beasts of England," many times over, for example. This feature also explains why the book can be read with pleasure by children, who no doubt identify more intensely than adults with the animals and their lack of total command of adult human skills. At the same time, the flattened characterizations suitable for animal allegory neutralize some of Orwell's special difficulties as a writer of fiction. He has at last found a framework in which authentic relationships between characters and insight into human beings—ordinary requirements of the novel—are simply not important.

Orwell's animal challenge to Marxism presupposes a unity among the animals (as among the humans) that is purely imaginary. Katharine Burdekin, in an extraordinary feminist novel entitled *Proud Man*, published in 1934 under the pseudonym "Murray Constantine," depicts British society from the vantage point of an evolved self-fertilizing "person" who refers to the rest of us as "subhumans." Burdekin's narrator states the matter in plain language: "A privilege of class divides a subhuman society horizontally, while a privilege of sex divides it vertically." Burdekin also discusses the problem of failed revolutions (which was later to preoccupy Orwell) and labels them "reversals of privilege." She relates these to the human preoccupation with the idea of importance, exacerbated in males due to their biological limitations—"womb envy," in short. In *Animal Farm*, however, Orwell does not address the vertical division of society—by sex— on which patriarchy rests. Of course, we know that his aim was to satirize "dictatorship in general" and the Russian Revolution in particular; but displacing his political message onto animals did not allow Orwell an avenue of escape from the messy business of the gender hierarchy. On the contrary, it is carefully reproduced in *Animal Farm*.

Although *Animal Farm* is mentioned in scores of studies of Orwell, no critic has thought it worth a comment that the pigs who betray the revolution, like the pig who starts it, are not just pigs but boars, that is, uncastrated male pigs kept for breeding purposes. Old Major, the "prize Middle White boar" (5) who has called a meeting to tell the other animals about his dream, is initially described in terms that establish him as patriarch of this world: "He was twelve years old and had lately grown rather stout, but he was still a majestic-looking pig, with a wise and benevolent appearance in spite of the fact that his tushes had never been cut" (5–6). In contrasting his life with those of the less fortunate animals on the farm, Major says: "I am one of the lucky ones. I am twelve years old and have had over four hundred children. Such is the natural life of a pig" (10). Orwell here repeats the pattern we have seen in his other fiction, of stressing paternity as if the actual labor of reproduction were done by males. Authority comes from the phallus and fatherhood, and the sows, in fact, are hardly mentioned in the book; when they are, as we shall see, it is solely to illustrate the patriarchal control of the ruling pig, Napoleon. Leaders, then, may be good (Major) or bad (Napoleon)—but they must be male and "potent."

Contrasting with the paternal principle embodied in Major is the maternal, embodied in Clover, "a stout motherly mare approaching middle life, who had never quite got her figure back after her fourth foal" (6). Clover is characterized above all by her nurturing concern for the other animals. When a brood of ducklings that had lost their mother come into the barn, Clover "made a sort of wall round them with her great foreleg," and they nestled down inside it (7). Though Clover works along with Boxer—the enormous cart horse "as strong as any two ordinary horses put together" (6) whom Orwell uses to represent the working class, unintelligent but ever-faithful, to judge by this image—she is admired not for her hard labor but rather for her caring role as protector of the weaker animals. Orwell here attributes to the maternal female dominion over the moral sphere but without any power to implement her values. As in *Nineteen Eighty-Four*, this "feminine" characteristic, though admirable, is shown to be utterly helpless and of no avail. In addition, this conventional (human) division of reality restricts the female animal to the affective and expressive sphere and the male to the instrumental.

Orwell at times utilizes the same imagery in opposing ways; imagery relating to passivity, for example, is presented as attractive in "Inside the Whale" and repulsive when associated with pansy pacifists. This ambivalence is demonstrated as well in Orwell's use of protective maternal imagery. Clover's protective gesture toward the ducklings, viewed positively in *Animal Farm*, is matched by Orwell's ridicule of a similar image in his verse polemic with Alex Comfort in 1943, about half a year before Orwell began composing *Animal Farm*. Falling into his familiar tough-guy rhetoric, Orwell angrily defended Churchill against pacifist gibes:

> But you don't hoot at Stalin—that's "not done"—
> Only at Churchill; I've no wish to praise him,
> I'd gladly shoot him when the war is won,
> Or now, if there were someone to replace him.
> But unlike some, I'll pay him what I owe him;
> There was a time when empires crashed like houses,
> And many a pink who'd titter at your poem
> Was glad enough to cling to Churchill's trousers.
> Christ! how they huddled up to one another
> Like day-old chicks about their foster-mother!
>
> [CEJL, 2:301]

The protective environment must (as in *Coming Up for Air*) be rejected if manly status is to be preserved. But the protective gesture itself, in its inevitable futility, is admired in *Animal Farm*, and it is through Clover that Orwell expresses the sadness of the failed revolution after the "purges" occur, as the stunned animals huddle around her:

> As Clover looked down the hillside her eyes filled with tears. If she could have spoken her thoughts, it would have been to say that this was not what they had aimed at when they had set them-selves years ago to work for the overthrow of the human race. These scenes of terror and slaughter were not what they had looked forward to on that night when old Major first stirred them to rebellion. If she herself had had any picture of the future, it had been of a society of animals set free from hunger and the

whip, all equal, each working according to his capacity, the strong protecting the weak, as she had protected the last brood of ducklings with her foreleg on the night of Major's speech. [75–76]

Clover is here contrasted with Boxer, who is unable to reflect on these matters and simply resolves to work even harder than before (74). Though Clover too "would remain faithful, work hard, carry out the orders that were given to her, and accept the leadership of Napoleon" (76), she has the moral awareness to know that "it was not for this that she and all the other animals had hoped and toiled" (76). But she lacks the words to express this awareness and instead sings "Beasts of England."

Clover stands at one of the poles of Orwell's conventional representation of female character. The other pole is represented by Mollie, "the foolish, pretty white mare who drew Mr Jones's trap" (7) and is shown, early in the book, to have a link with human females. When the animals wander through the farmhouse, Mollie lingers in the best bedroom: "She had taken a piece of blue ribbon from Mrs Jones's dressing-table, and was holding it against her shoulder and admiring herself in the glass in a very foolish manner" (21-22). A less important female character is the cat who, during Major's speech, finds the warmest place to settle down in and does not listen to a word he says (7). Both Mollie and the cat, we later learn, avoid work; and Mollie is the first defector from the farm after the revolution, seduced by a neighboring farmer's offerings of ribbons for her white mane and sugar.

Orwell's characterizations of old Major, Boxer, Clover, Mollie, and the cat all appear, clearly packaged and labeled, in the book's first three pages. The animal community thus forms a recognizable social world, divided by gender. This world is presented to us complete with stereotypes of patriarchal power, in the form of male wisdom, virility, or sheer strength, and female subordination, in the form of a conventional dichotomy between "good" maternal females and "bad" nonmaternal females. It is difficult to gauge Orwell's intentions in making use of gender stereotypes in *Animal Farm*. Given the evidence of his other texts, however, it seems unlikely that the possibility of a critical, even satirical, account of gender divisions ever crossed his mind. Perhaps he simply incorporated the familiar into his animal fable as part of the "natural human" traits needed to gain plausibility for his drama of a revolution betrayed. But in so doing he inadvertently reveals something very important about this barnyard revolution: Like its human counterparts, it invariably re-creates the institution of patriarchy.

Sexual Politics on the Farm

Not only does Orwell's satire of a Marxist ("Animalist") revolution fail to question gender domination while arguing against species domination, it actually depends upon the stability of patriarchy as an institution. This is demonstrated by the continuity between Mr. Jones, the original proprietor of the farm, and Napoleon (Stalin), the young boar who contrives to drive out Snowball (Trotsky), the only competing boar on the premises, and assumes Jones's former position as well as that of Major, the old patriarch.

In her study of feminism and socialism, Batya Weinbaum attempts to explain why socialist revolutions have tended to reestablish patriarchy. Describing this pattern in the Russian and Chinese revolutions, Weinbaum utilizes the terminology of kin categories: father, daughter, brother, wife. These categories allow her to point out that revolutions have expressed the revolt of brothers against fathers. Though her analysis relies on a Freudian model of sexual rivalry, agreement about motivation is not necessary in order to see the value of the kin categories she proposes. While daughters participate along with brothers in the early stages of revolution, they are increasingly left out of the centers of power once the brothers realize they can occupy the positions formerly held by the fathers, thus gaining privileged access to the labor and services of women.

It is intriguing to note how closely this scheme fits *Animal Farm*. Although Orwell describes a generalized revolt of the animals, inspired by a wise father's message of freedom, this revolt against the human exploiter Jones is quickly perverted into a struggle between two of the brothers, each eager to occupy the father slot and eliminate his competitor. Orwell makes it explicit that the struggle goes on between the only two boars among the pigs. The male porkers (castrated pigs) are not contenders for the father role. There is even an especially nasty portrayal of Squealer, the public relations porker who, in keeping with Orwell's other slurs against the press, is depicted as devoid of masculinity (in Orwell's terms): He stays safely away from the fighting. Once Napoleon wins out over Snowball, we see just what the father role means in terms of access to females. As the sole potent male pig on the farm, Napoleon is of course the father of the next generation of elite pigs: "In the autumn the four sows had all littered about simultaneously, producing thirty-one young pigs between them. The young pigs were piebald, and as Napoleon was the only boar on the farm, it was possible to guess at their parentage" (96).

In addition, the relations among the sows, competing for Napoleon's favor, are hinted at near the story's end, when Napoleon is on the verge of complete reconciliation with the human fathers, the neighboring farmers.

Orwell informs us that the pigs (males) began to wear Mr. Jones's clothes, "Napoleon himself appearing in a black coat, ratcatcher breeches, and leather leggings, while his favourite sow appeared in the watered silk dress which Mrs. Jones had been used to wearing on Sundays" (115). Perhaps because these details seem to be beside the point in terms of the allegory, they are all the more intriguing as instances of Orwell's fantasy at work. Intentionally or not, Orwell has re-created the structure of the patriarchal family. As in human families, power among the pigs is organized along two axes: sex and age.

Though we are told that the pigs as a whole exploit the other animals (by keeping more and better food for themselves, claiming exemption from physical labor because they are doing the "brainwork" of the farm, and finally moving into the farmhouse and adopting all the formerly proscribed human habits), it is only the male pigs whom we see, in the book's closing line, as indistinguishable from human males: "The creatures outside looked from pig to man, and from man to pig, and from pig to man again; but already it was impossible to say which was which" (120). Piggish adaptation to the human world involves not only the general class discrimination evident in the rewritten Commandment: "All animals are equal but some animals are more equal than others" (114). It also appears more specifically in the gender hierarchy that culminates in this last scene, so different from the account of the revolution itself in which virtually all the animals and both sexes had participated.

Even as the animal allegory duplicates Orwell's gender assumptions, it also liberates him to some extent from the confines of his own androcentric framework. This is apparent in the unfolding of old Major's speech early in the book. He begins with general comments about the animals' lot: "No animal in England knows the meaning of happiness or leisure after he is a year old. No animal in England is free. The life of an animal is misery and slavery: that is the plain truth" (8). But as he continues to speak, his emphasis shifts slightly:

> Why then do we continue in this miserable condition? Because nearly the whole of our produce is stolen from us by human beings. There, comrades, is the answer to all our problems. It is summed up in a single word—Man. Man is the only real enemy we have. Remove Man from the scene, and the root cause of hunger and overwork is abolished forever.
>
> Man is the only creature that consumes without producing. He does not give milk, he does not lay eggs, he is too weak to pull the plough, he cannot run fast enough to catch rabbits. [8–9]

Here, for the first and only time in his writings, Orwell recognizes female reproductive labor as part and parcel of a society's productive activities and as a form of labor that gives females the right to make political and economic demands. In old Major's speech, it is this female labor, specifically, that becomes the most dramatic focal point. The passage quoted above continues:

> Yet he [Man] is lord of all the animals. He sets them to work, he gives back to them the bare minimum that will prevent them from starving, and the rest he keeps for himself. Our labour tills the soil, our dung fertilizes it, and yet there is not one of us that owns more than his bare skin. You cows that I see before me, how many thousands of gallons of milk have you given during this last year? And what has happened to that milk which should have been breeding up sturdy calves? Every drop of it has gone down the throats of our enemies. And you hens, how many eggs have you laid this year, and how many of those eggs ever hatched into chickens? The rest have all gone to market to bring in money for Jones and his men. And you, Clover, where are those four foals you bore, who should have been the support and pleasure of your old age? Each was sold at a year old—you will never see one of them again. In return for your four confinements and all your labour in the field, what have you ever had except your bare rations and a stall? [9]

In this passage Orwell is finally able to make the connection between "public" and "private"—between the male's (typical) work of production and the female's (typical) work of reproduction. He sees that both forms of labor can be expropriated and that the "private" sphere in which relations of caring and nurturing go on is very much a part of the overall system of exploitation that old Major protests. Thinking about animals, Orwell notices that females are insufficiently rewarded for the labor stolen from them by men.

As the revolution decays, there occurs an episode in which Napoleon forces the hens to give up more of their eggs, so that they can be used for export to a neighboring farm. At first the hens sabotage this plan by dropping their eggs from the rafters of the barn. But they are quickly brought into line by the cessation of their rations (the acquisition of food still not being under their direct control). After holding out for five days, the hens capitulate (66–67). This increased expropriation of the hens' products is viewed by Orwell in precisely the same terms as the increased labor time extracted from the other animals. In contrast, when Orwell wrote about the human working class, he never noticed the economics of reproduction or objected to women's exclusion from direct access to decent livelihoods—an exclusion justified by reference to their status as females and supposed dependents of males. It is as if, since his farm animals are not divided into individual family groupings, Orwell was able to break through the ideology of "typical family" that had earlier blinded him to the reality of women's work and position in capitalist society.

In *Animal Farm*, furthermore, Orwell touches on the problem of political expropriation of female reproductive capacity. Napoleon provides himself with a secret police force by separating a litter of newborn puppies from their mothers and rearing them himself, and these puppies, when grown up, drive out the rival brother, Snowball, and inaugurate Napoleon's reign of terror. Orwell here seems to protest against the breakup of the "natural" pattern by which the pups are suckled and raised by their mothers. This theme is reiterated when Napoleon seizes the thirty-one young pigs—his offspring—and appoints himself their instructor, so as to prepare the continued domination of pigs over the other animals in the future. Such "unnatural" expropriations stand in sharp opposition to the traditional patterns of family life so strongly supported by Orwell. The same sort of "state" interference in family life occurs, in more detailed form, in *Nineteen Eighty-Four*.

Although his fiction suggests a strong distaste for these examples of state expropriation of female reproductive labor, Orwell was actually urging the adoption in England of population policies that, if put into practice, would have openly treated women as mere vehicles for fulfilling state priorities. In "The English People," written in 1944 (that is, shortly after *Animal Farm*) though not published until 1947, Orwell, in the throes of a panic about the dwindling birthrate, exhorts the English to have more children as one of the necessary steps in order to "retain their vitality" (CEJL, 3:31). Interpreting the declining birthrate primarily as an economic problem, he urges the government to take appropriate measures:

> Any government, by a few strokes of the pen, could make child-lessness as unbearable an economic burden as a big family is now: but no government has chosen to do so, because of the ignorant idea that a bigger population means more unemployed. Far more drastically than anyone has proposed hitherto, taxation will have to be graded so as to encourage child-bearing and to save women with young children from being obliged to work outside the home. [3:32]

In addition to economic and social incentives, Orwell says, a "change of outlook" is needed: "In the England of the last thirty years it has seemed all too natural that blocks of flats should refuse tenants with children, that parks and squares should be railed off to keep the children out of them, that abortion, theoretically illegal, should be looked on as a peccadillo, and that the main aim of commercial advertising should be to popularise the idea of 'having a good time' and staying young as long as possible" (3:32).

In brief, what the English must do is, among other things, to "breed faster, work harder, and probably live more simply" (3:37), a program ominously reminiscent of Napoleon's exhortation to the other animals: "The truest happiness, he said, lay in working hard and living frugally" (*Animal Farm*, 109). In Orwell's concern with socially adequate human breeding there is no more consideration for the choices of women than Napoleon shows for the desires of the hens or bitches whose eggs and puppies he removes. Orwell seems to assume that the "natural" desires of women will precisely coincide with the lines he sets out—if, that is, he has paused to look at the matter from their point of view at all. Several years later, Orwell still viewed the "population problem" in the same terms. In a newspaper column in 1947, he voices alarm that, if England does not quickly reach an average family size of four children (instead of the then existing average of two), "there will not be enough women of child-bearing age to restore the situation." He worries about where future workers will come from and again recommends financial incentives. Though Orwell was hardly alone in expressing such concerns at that time, it is instructive to note the limited perspective he brings to the problem. And yet in *Nineteen Eighty-Four* he satirizes the Party's control over Outer Party members' reproductive behavior through the character of Winston's wife, Katharine, who chills Winston's blood with her commitment to regular sexual intercourse as an expression of "our duty to the Party." It seems obvious that Orwell's opinion of such state interference in sex and procreation has nothing to do with any sympathy for women as individuals but depends entirely upon his judgment of the merits of the state that is being served.

Nothing in Orwell's earlier writings reveals an awareness of the economic contributions made by women as reproducers, rearers, and caretakers of the labor force, not to mention as ordinary members of the work force. It is therefore all the more surprising that in letting his imagination translate human conflicts into animal terms this aspect of female roles at once sprang to his attention. At the same time, his female animals are still rudimentary in comparison with the more subtly drawn portraits of the male animals on the farm. The hens and cows, for example, appear primarily as good followers, prefiguring Orwell's description of Outer Party female supporters in *Nineteen Eighty-Four*. With the exception of the maternal

Clover and, to a lesser extent, Mollie, the female animals are unimportant as individual actors in the fable.

The animals are differentiated not only according to gender but also by intelligence, the pigs being described as both intelligent and piggish even at an early stage in the revolution, when they appropriate the cows' milk for their own use. The other animals, with only a few exceptions, are generous, hardworking, and stupid by contrast. It is not power that corrupts the pigs; power simply provides them with the means to realize their "nature." The betrayal of the revolution in *Animal Farm*, though it occurs over a period of time, is not, in fact, described as a process. This is why *Animal Farm*, beyond what it has to say concerning Stalin and the Soviet Union, has a profoundly dispiriting message. Orwell presents a static picture of a static universe in which the notion of the pigs' animal nature explains what happens. The final tableau, with the pigs and the men indistinguishable, is the actualization of the potential inherent in the pigs from the beginning. Unlike what he does in *Nineteen Eighty-Four*, however, Orwell gives the pigs specific material motives for the exploitation of the other animals: better food, more leisure, and a privileged life, all acquired partly by terrorizing and partly by gulling the others into thinking that because the pigs are more intelligent they alone can manage the farm. The question of intelligence is a problematic one in this book, for Orwell associates this characteristic with exploitation. There is a suggestion here that generosity, cooperation, devotion are somehow incompatible with intelligence. The deeper question, of what power hunger is really about, is avoided, and the apparent answers Orwell provides in his animal fable are inconsistent and unsatisfying, for even among the pigs not all are shown to be corrupted by greed and the desire for power.

As the pigs duplicate the human model of social organization, they not only reproduce the pattern of patriarchy already familiar to the animals (judging by Major's status early in the book) but add to it those human characteristics that Orwell found most reprehensible—especially softness. They slowly adopt Mr. Jones's manner of living, complete with cushy bed and booze. This is contrasted with the heroic labor of the immensely strong Boxer, who literally works himself to death. Relations between the pigs and the other animals follow the patriarchal model also in that they are hierarchical and discipline-oriented; submission and obedience are extracted from the worker animals as the price of the supposedly indispensable pig leadership.

In addition to the touching solidarity evident among the worker animals, some individual relationships also emerge. One of these is the nonverbal "masculine" friendship between Boxer and Benjamin, who look forward to their retirement together. There is no female version of this friendship, however. Instead, Clover plays the role not only of maternal mare to the other animals but also of "wife"—to use Weinbaum's kin categories again—in that she has a heart-to-heart talk with Mollie. Cast in the role of the rebellious "daughter" who refuses to adhere to the farm's values, Mollie disbelieves in the communal cause and prefers to ally herself with powerful human males outside the farm, thus assuring her easier life as a kept and well-decorated mare. Orwell signals his disapproval of Mollie by showing her cowardice (39) as well as her vanity and sloth. Given the revolution's eventual outcome, however, Mollie's behavior, though egocentric, is not as misguided as it may seem. Orwell makes it explicit that under the rule of Napoleon the animals (except the pigs and Moses, the raven, who represents the church) have an even more arduous work life than animals on the neighboring (i.e., capitalist) farms. Mollie might better be viewed as having some spontaneous understanding of the rules of patriarchy, characterized by Weinbaum in these words: "Brothers may step across the line to become fathers; but daughters face a future as a powerless wife."

Animal Farm as a Feminist Fable

With astonishing ease and aptness, *Animal Farm* can be read as a feminist critique of socialist revolutions which, through their failure to challenge patriarchy, have reproduced patriarchal values in the postrevolutionary period. In this reading of the fable, the pigs would be the sole male animals, while most of the other animals are stereotyped females: compliant, hardworking drones brainwashed with the illusion that their work is done for themselves, surrendering the fruits of their productive and reproductive labor to their masters, who tell them that there never was hope of a different future.

As in the power relations between men and women, so in *Animal Farm* "science" is used to explain that pigs need better and bigger rations because they are "brain workers," an argument offering the additional message that the dependent animals could not manage on their own. These brainworkers take on the "hard" work of supervising the political and economic life of the farm, consigning the rest to the "less important" tasks of physical labor and maintenance of the farm/home. By also assuming the burden of "international" relations (with neighboring farms), the pigs keep the others pure from any contaminating contact with the outside world—again, an uncanny parallel to the public/private split of ordinary patriarchal society. Whether the individual nonpig animal is big and strong like Boxer or small and weak like the hens, it is held in check by an ideology of its own ignorance and dependence, subjected to violence and intimidation, and urged to sacrifice itself. Such an animal is not likely to rebel. But, as Orwell himself pointed out, the book does not end on a totally pessimistic note. For in the recognition that pigs and men are identical lies the spark of knowledge that can lead to liberatory action.

It would be absurd, of course, to suggest that Orwell intended such a feminist reading of his text. Everything he ever wrote shows that he took the patriarchal family to be the proper model of society. In "The Lion and the Unicorn" he complained only that England was like "a family with the wrong members in control,"

> a rather stuffy Victorian family, with not many black sheep in it but with all its cupboards bursting with skeletons. It has rich relations who have to be kow-towed to and poor relations who are horribly sat upon, and there is a deep conspiracy of silence about the source of the family income. It is a family in which the young are generally thwarted and most of the power is in the hands of irresponsible uncles and bedridden aunts. Still, it is a family. It has its private language and its common memories, and at the approach of an enemy it closes its ranks. [CEJL, 2:68]

Of course, Orwell's version of just who is in control itself indicates his habitual misreading of the status of women in his own society. It seems to me that Orwell's complaint was on behalf of the brothers alone, as evidenced by his lack of awareness of the real disunity inherent in the patriarchal family.

It is fascinating to see Orwell describe the betrayal of the animals' revolution in terms so suggestive of women's experience under patriarchy. It is women who, more than any other group and regardless of the race and class to which they belong, have had their history obliterated, their words suppressed and forgotten, their position in society confounded by the doublethink of "All men are created equal," their legal rights denied, their labor in the home and outside of it expropriated and controlled by men, their reproductive capacities used against them, their desire for knowledge thwarted, their strivings turned into dependence—all of these under the single pretext that they are not "by nature" equipped to do the valued work of society, defined as what men do. When read as a feminist fable, however, *Animal Farm* has another important message. The origins of the Seven Commandments of Animalism lie in Major's warnings against adopting Man's ways: "And remember also that in fighting against Man, we must not come to resemble him. Even when you have conquered him, do not adopt his vices" (11–12).

Orwell knew that something was missing from his political analysis, however, as is apparent in one of his "As I Please" columns dating from November 1946, in which he examines the front page of a daily newspaper and deplores the typical disasters it records. Long recovered from the quietist mood of "Inside the Whale" but now deeply pessimistic, he writes: "I think one must continue the political struggle, just as a doctor must try to save the life of a patient who is probably going to die. But I do suggest that we shall get nowhere unless we start by recognising that political behaviour is largely non-rational, that the world is suffering from some kind of mental disease which must be diagnosed before it can be cured" (CEJL, 4:248–49). *Nineteen Eighty-Four* can help us to understand the nature of this illness.

PATRICK REILLY

The Utopian Shipwreck

No one can miss the striking difference in mood, style and content between Orwell's last two books, the first playfully ready to take its place alongside such established children's classics as *Gulliver's Travels* and *Treasure Island*, the other bleak with the chill of irremediable defeat. How could such *élan* and such misery follow so close upon each other?

The difficulty seems less when one reflects that the allegory is almost as pessimistic as the prophecy, equally depressing in its conclusions, and that only its very specialised form obscures this, persuading us to rejoice in a record of disillusion disguised as a fairy tale. *Animal Farm* succeeds to the degree that it disciplines its subject matter and subdues life to art, taming terror to the requirements of a beast fable. It is humorous so long as we see animals and forget men, as the genre so obligingly enables us to do.

Nevertheless, it is no surprise to find the old, troublesome questions of humankind arising in field and barn: power and righteousness, freedom and order, and the difficulty, perhaps impossibility, of harmonising them; to find, too, since it is Orwell, the intractable problem of mortality again presenting itself—no other single item so conclusively reveals the human bedrock of the animal fable. The pigs, proselytising for a revolution which may still be life-times away, are challenged by some of the animals to justify self-sacrifice now: 'Why should we care what happens after we are dead?' (*Animal Farm*,

From *George Orwell: The Age's Adversary*. © 1986 by Patrick Reilly.

p. 16). Once again it is the old vexed problem of lost immortality. For the pigs the question is stupid, since the philosophy of Animalism is so unarguably the answer; but, when Animalism itself is exposed as simply another swindle, the questioners have every right to feel unanswered, if not cheated. That Moses can still peddle Sugarcandy on the allegedly liberated farm is, on Marxist premises, sufficient proof that Animalism has failed, since a true philosophy must, in abolishing misery and want, simultaneously eliminate the dream of heaven. If the dream still survives, this alone proves that the just society is still to seek; attacking religion is as sensible as smashing the barometer when the weather is bad.

That the dream of the just society had long dominated Orwell's thought the essay on Koestler makes plain. Discussing Koestler's novel *The Gladiators*, Orwell comments that the dream haunts the human imagination ineradicably and in all ages, whether in the form of the kingdom of Heaven or in that of the classless society (*CEJL*, III, 274). Writing in 1946 he declared that his ambition for ten years past had been to make political writing into an art. The ambition was, however, unceasingly regulated by a moral impulse (I, 28). When aesthetic perfection wrestles with the demands of justice, Orwell unfailingly sides with the latter. If, as Eliot says, the progress of an artist is a continual self-sacrifice, a continual extinction of personality, one must conclude that Orwell had not advanced much in these ten years. Orwell inherits from Swift the urge to expose and vex the world, but lacks the artistic detachment of his great predecessor—indignation (we have his own word for it) was always liable to disturb the artist's poise.

Homage to Catalonia is an illuminating instance. The strain of writing it solely with a strict regard for form finally proved too great: a long chapter of newspaper quotations, defending the hunted POUM against their Communist persecutors, gatecrashes the book, irretrievably violating its formal qualities. Orwell admits the offence against art, concedes the ephemerality of the interpolation, and accepts the judgement of a respected critic that he had reduced a good book to journalism. Yet he is unrepentant: 'I could not have done otherwise', he says (*CEJL*, I, 29)—did he realise he was echoing Luther?

Truth is Orwell's compulsion: innocent men were being vilified and murdered—unable to save their lives, he resolved to defend their reputations, not maintain a shameful silence for the sake of aesthetic purity. An art procuring its perfection over the bones of the innocent makes its practitioner the literary analogue of Macbeth. As the essay on Dali makes plain, Orwell abhorred the doctrine that exalts aesthetic delight above decency (III, 189–95; IV, 552). The new aesthetic version of benefit of clergy evoked his unqualified disapproval: a wall good by the mason's criteria is an abomination to be flattened when it surrounds a concentration camp—the better the structure, the worse the outrage.

Dali's skill has enlisted under decadence, and Orwell will no more absolve such art than Lord Longford forgive a pornographer of genius. The cinema audience of *Nineteen Eighty-Four* bursts into spontaneous, appreciative applause at 'a wonderful shot of a child's arm going up up up right up into the air', and later in the book an aesthete of hangings discusses the items that please him most: the legs kicking (it spoils it when the feet are tied), 'and, above all, at the end, the tongue sticking right out, and blue—a quite bright blue. That's the detail that appeals to me' (p. 11, p. 43). Orwell's overriding priority is the relief of human suffering—he would have preferred to stop someone falling to death than obtain a camera scoop of the descent, for he loved men more than art. To prove this we need not cite his denunciation of the sophisticated cosmopolitan scum who gave Dali his livelihood or point to his preference for the rude, healthy rustics who inhabit Tolstoy's pages (*CEJL*, III, 129). No need either to recall his condemnation of Ezra Pound's speeches for Mussolini: 'One has the right to expect ordinary decency of a poet' (III, 106). Joyce is the decisive test, for among modern writers he loved Joyce best. Yet, revering the artist, he could rebuke the man. Even Joyce, seeking to be a 'pure' artist, indifferent to politics, should see that stupidity is preferable to totalitarianism, Anglo-Irish philistinism, however crass, to Hitler (III, 131). Nobody can be above the battle of the twentieth century, because not just a political system or even a civilisation is threatened, but the crystal spirit itself, the fragile essence of man, hitherto complacently deemed inviolable, in truth as vulnerable as the shattered paperweight of *Nineteen Eight-Four.*

Gide may insist that the aesthetic point of view is the only one to take in in discussing his work, but Orwell will sacrifice art itself when life is in the other scale. This is the core of his achievement, and a concern for life is not so abundant, especially in our century, that we can afford to sniff at it. We, for our part, must ungrudgingly pay its price and not demand from the fervent truth-teller the cool detachment that a writer with more art and less mission might supply. 'Aesthetic scrupulousness is not enough, but political rectitude is not enough either' (*CEJL*, II, 153). In one book alone, as he himself recognised, did Orwell successfully integrate reformer and artist: '*Animal Farm* was the first book in which I tried, with full consciousness of what I was doing, to fuse political purpose and artistic purpose into one whole' (I, 29). In every other book we sense his active presence; here alone he realises Stephen Dedalus's ideal of the invisible creator and forsakes the easily detected ventriloquisms of earlier fictions. Ironically, it is the triumph of this disappearing-act that creates some of the most disconcerting problems for the reader.

The artistic triumph is inseparable from the chosen form; its good humour and equanimity stem from its status as animal fable. It was initially rejected by American publishers on the ground that there was no market for animal stories (IV, 138). We smile at a judgement so childishly blind to the allegorical import, yet this in itself is a tribute to the art. There is, in any case, something decisive about the Aesopian base: the choice of animals rather than human beings gave Orwell for the first time a certain latitude, release from that sense of moral constraint that otherwise held him captive, driving him to violate knowingly the unity of *Homage to Catalonia*, soliciting his own intervention throughout other books. The liberating secret lay in making animals behave like men.

Men behaving like animals, if comic at all, makes for a comedy verging on nightmare, that of *Volpone* or *Gulliver's Travels*—the Yahoos alarm us not as beasts but as brothers, for Gulliver's shocking discovery is that beneath his European disguise he is a 'perfect Yahoo'. Animals behaving like men are, by contrast, inherently funny, the fact so assiduously exploited by Walt Disney —even the villainous tiger of *The Jungle Book* has proved irresistible to generations of delighted children. 'Some fool has said that one cannot hate an animal; he should try a few nights in India, when the dogs are baying the moon' (*Burmese Days*, p. 59). But this is the frantic Flory speaking, a man whose love-affair with instability ends in suicide. The 'fool' he rebukes is in fact right; *Animal Farm* is so exuberantly successful because one cannot hate an animal, not even when the animal is Napoleon, a nasty pig who is farm-yard stand-in for a monstrous dictator.

The very style of the fable tames catastrophe through levity, resolves terror in comedy. In life Orwell dreaded totalitarian propaganda as the supreme iniquity of our time, the throttling of truth even as a theoretic possibility; in the art of *Animal Farm* the image of a pig up a ladder with a paintbrush alchemises the horror into humour, putting Orwell and the reader in serene control of the situation. If the other animals are taken in by Squealer's impudent trickery, so much the worse for them—the reader isn't such a fool, and when he laughs at the bungled cheat he simultaneously proclaims his happy superiority to it. Material unbearable in life becomes in art a source of comic delight. When the newly liberated animals, obedient to the first duties of the victors, bring out the hams from Jones's kitchen to enact the solemn ritual of interment, the reader is invited to smile rather than mourn (*Animal Farm*, p. 22). Orwell's burial of the dead has nothing in common with T. S. Eliot's.

In a book where comedy rules, it is fitting that Jones should be chased off the farm with no more than a few butts and kicks, that, after his pride, his backside is the most serious casualty of the Battle of the Cowshed.

Admittedly, his eventual death in alcoholic delirium is horrific enough, but it is self-inflicted, and, like the catastrophes of classical drama, occurs off-stage. The fable is inhospitable to anything resembling the ghastly conclusion in the cellar at Ekaterinburg—the reader would be revolted at the Joneses trampled to death under the horses' hooves or devoured by the dogs. We only hear that Jones has children because of the old discarded spelling-book which the pigs rescue from the rubbish heap in order to learn to read. In fact the Czar's children, not their primer, were flung on the rubbish heap, but the fable softens reality. Orwell insists on a victimless revolution. When, later, the men invade the farm, Orwell will not allow any of them to be killed in the successful counterattack. Boxer's massive hoof catches a stable lad on the skull, leaving him apparently 'stretched . . . lifeless in the mud' (p. 38). But here too there is the same welcome reassurance as in *The Tempest*: 'Tell your piteous heart/There's no harm done' (I.ii. 15–16).

Boxer's solicitude is upheld against Snowball's ferocity. Pawing grief-stricken at the inert body, Boxer is rebuked by the pig for his sentimentality: 'War is war. The only good human being is a dead one' (*Animal Farm*, p. 39). Orwell knows how insidiously easy it is to become infected with war fever: 'I do think it is a dreadful effect of war that one is actually pleased to hear of an enemy sub going to the bottom' (*CEJL*, II, 409). He feared the temptation of vindictiveness the more because he had experienced the emotion in himself: 'That bastard Chiappe is cold meat. Everyone delighted, as when Balbo died. This war is at any rate killing off a few Fascists' (II, 431). From this, if unchecked, it is a straight descent to the cinema audience of *Nineteen Eighty-Four* enjoying the newsreels of 'enemy' women and children being strafed by planes from Airstrip One. But Boxer in the audience would not be rejoicing. Even human life is precious to him; he has no enemies that he wants dead—his human equivalent will not be found administering the Gulag or Auschwitz—and, Snowball's jungle realism notwithstanding, his eyes are full of tears. Orwell plainly sides with the horse.

In any case, Snowball is wrong, factually as well as morally: this is *not* war, but is limited, at Orwell's insistence, to cuts and bruises. The animals leave to search for the missing Mollie and when they return the stable lad has scampered—he has merely been stunned: 'the child is not dead but sleepeth'. Orwell vetoes extreme violence, whether by men against animals or animals against men; when, finally, it does erupt, it is ironically inflicted by animals upon animals, not because Orwell wishes it so, but because this is the tragedy which even the comic fable cannot conceal.

Nevertheless, it is crucially decisive that the tragedy happens to and among animals. The reader *knows* everything in *Animal Farm*—it is the animals who are forever mystified right up to the final bewildering metamorphosis. In *Nineteen Eighty-Four*, by contrast, the reader is left in the same perplexed anguish as Winston with Goldstein's exegesis still unread. Like distraught Othello, the reader and Winston both know how but not why.

> Will you, I pray, demand that demi-devil
> Why he hath thus ensnared my soul and body?

Nineteen Eighty-Four is as resolute as Iago in not providing an answer:

> Demand me nothing; what you know, you know;
> From this time forth I never will speak word.

The object of all the sadism in Oceania is, it seems, simply more sadism, sadism as an end in itself; Iago and Big Brother like being nasty. This aspect of *Nineteen Eighty-Four* will always strike some readers as unsatisfactory, a species of twentieth-century *grand guignol*, in which author as well as book surrender to the mysticism of cruelty. It is a charge that could never be made against *Animal Farm*. There, apart from a possible irritation at being forced to choose between Napoleon and Boxer (the available options within the text are unacceptable, while the acceptable option is not available), the reader is always in control of the fable. The villain of *Animal Farm*, unlike those of Othello or *Nineteen Eighty-Four*, is always pellucidly open, often derisively so—we never *fear* Napoleon as we do Iago and Big Brother. The reader is in the superior position of a sophisticated onlooker at a country fair watching a bunch of yokels being taken in by a third-rate charlatan. Orwell castrates terror in the comic spectacle of an allegedly teetotal pig suffering from a hangover and swearing, like the rest of us, never to do it again. It is a scene not from the world of totalitarian terror, of Hitler and Stalin, purges and camps, but from that of Donald McGill, of mothers-in-law, dirty weekends and marital squabbles.

Naturally, the animals take a very different view of things, but the reader sees Napoleon less as a ferocious tyrant than as a comic cheat whose inept attempts at duplicity provoke laughter rather than indignation. When human tyrants suffer hangovers, they presumably become more fearful as the executions mount with the migraines. Forced to identify with Winston, we fear Big Brother, and rightly, for our lives hang upon his whims. In *Nineteen Eighty-Four* the reader is included *in* the diminishing-technique, which makes him an insignificant bug like Winston, liable at any instant to be squashed into unpersonhood. In *Animal Farm*, by contrast, the reader is serenely above the diminution, watching with amused immunity the terrifying tale of contemporary history scaled to Lilliputian proportions, tamed to the level of a barnyard fable. The prophecy magnifies the tyrant and diminishes the reader; the allegory magnifies the reader and diminishes the tyrant.

Orwell knew from personal experience how thoroughly dislikable pigs could be: 'The pig has grown to a stupendous size and goes to the butcher next week. We are all longing to get rid of him, as he is so destructive and greedy, even gets into the kitchen at times' (*CEJL*, IV, 518). In life the troublesome pig goes to the butcher; in the nightmare fairy tale the pig decides who goes to the butcher and is not just occasionally in the kitchen but in unchallengeable control of the house itself. But the trivialisation implicit in the fable form necessarily keeps the reader superior and secure.

All the events are deliberately diminished. The suppression of the kulaks in the Ukraine is reduced to a rebellion of hens at the sale of their eggs; it ends with nine hens starved to death—the fable's equivalent of the millions of peasants who died in the aftermath of Stalin's victory (*Animal Farm*, p. 67). Swift in Lilliput similarly trivialises the wars of the Reformation to an absurd wrangle between Big- and Little-Endians. Orwell employs the same technique to exchange the harrowing emotions provoked by twentieth-century history for an Olympian poise, so making the events easier to handle. The allegations of industrial sabotage which issued in the Moscow showcase trials dwindle into a broken window and a blocked drain, while treason to the Revolution finds its appropriate image in a sheep urinating in a drinking-pool (p. 73).

The most amusingly 'domestic' of these substitutions is the account of Mollie's defection. We hear that she is becoming 'more and more troublesome', and there are rumours of 'something more serious' than her habitual giddiness (p. 41). What Marcuse deplores as the seduction of large sections of the Western working class, bribed by the titbits of consumerism, is here depicted in terms of the fallen woman of Victorian melodrama, as Mollie goes down the well-worn road of Little Em'ly and Hetty Sorrel. The matronly Clover does her best to save the wanton—she is accepting sugar and ribbons from the men, has even been caught in *flagrante delicto* allowing her nose to be stroked—but the attempted rescue is as futile as Mrs Poyser's remonstrations. The last the scandalised animals hear is that Mollie is traipsing about town with a vulgar publican; after this, 'none of the animals ever mentioned Mollie again' (p. 42). The shame of the lapse is emphasized in the best Victorian tradition. When the animals metaphorically turn Mollie's face to the wall, the reader applauds the reductive wit, and, in his amusement, necessarily neglects the seriousness of the defection as viewed from Marcuse's perspective.

In becoming a Brobdingnagian, the reader finds it increasingly difficult to take these Lilliputian vanities with anything other than delight, amusement, perhaps a touch of contempt, much as Gulliver's giant hosts took him. Napoleon urinating on the windmill blueprint recalls Gulliver dousing Lilliputian fires, with Treaty of Utrecht and Five Year Plan alike finding their satiric value in a bladder evacuation. It is the identical technique that Swift consistently employs throughout the *Travels* and *The Tale*. When Walpole's chicanery is represented by Lilliputian ropedancers or Henry IV's projected invasion of the Empire likened to a bully throwing stones at a whore's window, the purpose anticipates Orwell's: to control a material which, taken at its everyday estimate and customary magnification, would cause the writer pain, alarm and indignation. Small is masterable; when Stalin becomes a pig and Europe a farmyard, the nightmare of contemporary history is transmuted, through the power of art, into a blithe and inspired fantasy.

Thus to criticise Orwell for allegedly demeaning the common people by depicting them as moronically credulous brutes is to misread the book. The animal fable is devised not to insult the ordinary man but to distance Orwell from the terror: existence becomes endurable as an aesthetic phenomenon. Schiller argues that only in art is man free. Mann described his Joseph tetralogy, written between 1926 and 1943 (the period covered by Orwell's fable), as his attempt to escape the horror by burying himself in an innocent and serene creation of the Spirit. Simplicity is an essential part of Orwell's disarming strategy. *Animal Farm*, as its subtitle 'A Fairy Tale' makes plain, is a convenient simplification, yet its simplicity came hard: 'the only one of my books I really sweated over'. Orwell's efforts were fully justified. Burckhardt had prophesied the coming of the terrible simplifiers, and the totalitarian men of the twentieth century vindicated the insight. *Animal Farm* is Orwell's response, a countersimplification designed to contain and disarm the frightful annals of modern Europe. 'You cannot take a purely aesthetic interest in a disease you are dying from' (*CEJL*, II, 152). The terminal atmosphere of the death ward pervades *Nineteen Eighty-Four*; *Animal Farm*, by contrast, presents its dark medicine in the form of a gay and fanciful fable.

The decision establishes the style of comic control, which Orwell only occasionally deserts to inject a more exalted, more sombre, sometimes more chilling note into the tale. His own unquestionable commitment to the revolutionary ideal is reflected in the elevated style with which he describes the morning after liberation and the sentiments of the triumphant animals. As they survey the familiar landscape in 'the clear morning light' of the new dispensation's first dawn, existence suddenly becomes a festival newly appreciated: 'it was as though they had never seen these things before' (*Animal Farm*, p. 21). Behold, I make all things new. The fun is momentarily forgotten in the high emotional contagion of the revolutionary hope.

Nor is there any fun, though for a very different reason, in the description of the stunned reaction to Snowball's flight from Napoleon's dogs: 'silent and terrified, the animals crept back into the barn' (p. 48). All the levity vanishes with the vanished Snowball, yet even this incident is merely a rehearsal for the climactic horror of the purges. As soon as the accused pigs confess, 'the dogs promptly tore their throats out' (p. 73)—the fate which Jones is not allowed to suffer. The bloodletting continues: hens, pigs, sheep 'were all slain on the spot. And so the tale of confessions and executions went on, until there was a pile of corpses lying before Napoleon's feet and the air was heavy with the smell of blood, which had been unknown there since the expulsion of Jones' (p. 74). No longer can the reader smile, for the weight of that blood-impregnated air presses heavy upon him too, as Napoleon becomes Moloch. The mood here is much closer: to the Miniluv chapters of *Nineteen Eighty-Four* than to the Aesopian fable that has hitherto charmed us.

Hard upon the scene of blood comes the pastoral scene when the stricken animals retreat into the beauty of the landscape to reprieve their shattered spirits. Yet this very beauty has taken on a plangent heartbreaking quality: 'as Clover looked upon the hillside her eyes filled with tears' (*Animal Farm*, p. 75). The serene landscape and the high utopian aspirations consort so ill with the recent carnage that all Clover can do is weep, while Boxer hauls stones to stupefy himself.

At the opening of the final chapter Orwell employs yet another style to evoke a mood of elegiac intensity: 'Years passed. The seasons came and went, the short animal lives fled by. A time came when there was no one who remembered the old days before the Rebellion. . . . Muriel was dead; Bluebell, Jessie and Pincher were dead . . .' (p. 108). It is the same melancholic chord that sounds through 'Dover Beach', bringing 'the eternal note of sadness in'; and it is a tribute to the flexibility of Orwell's style that the book can accommodate such diverse moods, be hospitable to comedy, pathos and satire without pulling itself apart.

Nevertheless, joy is the paramount emotion of the book, and the delight of the creative imagination in so triumphantly alchemising the sordid materials which are its datum—we have art, says Nietzsche, that we may not perish of the truth—is irrepressibly there from the opening paragraph when the drunken farmer lurches to bed, 'with the ring of light from his lantern dancing from side to side' (p. 5). No sooner is his bedroom light extinguished than the farm leaps to life, with a 'stirring' and a 'fluttering' all through its animal quarters. While the humans snore in heedless, intoxicated irresponsibility, the animal world is vibrantly awake, and the book mimics the lantern in the dance which it initiates and sustains; the book dances with the lantern, is a dancing-book as no other book of Orwell's is. We search in vain for a parallel opening throughout Orwell, will not find it even in *Homage to Catalonia*, that similar record of heady revolution modulating into entrapment. The characteristic Orwellian opening is more akin to that of *The Waste Land* than to that of *The Canterbury Tales*; we need only recall our first encounter with Dorothy Hare or Gordon Comstock or Winston Smith, the bleak mood and the depressing atmosphere, the little life fed with dried tubers, the rancour, spleen and misery—not much dancing there. *Animal Farm*, by contrast, begins in gaiety, and, even as it moves towards disenchantment, the joy is never entirely lost or forgotten.

The great experiment must, of course, begin in elation because its end is disillusion. Yet Old Major's dream of the elusively just society, submit though it must to the scrutiny of reason and the probings of scepticism, is not one that the book commends us to discard as worthless or obsolete. To settle for the world's injustice as ineluctably given, a datum of existence at which only fools will cavil, ranges one compromisingly with the knaves who urge the 'wisdom' of acceptance to justify their own depravities. Orwell himself never ceased to dream, however guardedly and with prophylactic self-derision, of the just society which he had seen flower briefly in Barcelona; like Gramsci, he combined pessimism of the intelligence with optimism of the will. Because things are not as we wish doesn't entail capitulation to them as they are: if we cannot get what we like, must we like what we get? If freedom is a dream, must we love the jailer?

The fool-knave antithesis of *Animal Farm* frustrates any simple solution to the problem. To stress the animals' folly in believing in justice comes perilously close to the knavish position that amendment is a delusion and exploitation a destiny. Boxer is so egregiously a fool because the pigs are so blatantly rogues. We may mock Gulliver's project to reform the Yahoos only by certifying ourselves as incurable. Similarly, if we use *Animal Farm* to dismiss the just society as moonshine, we vindicate our intelligence only at the price of publishing its porcine nature.

Intelligence and decency, power and righteousness, are irreconcilably opposed throughout the book. The good animals are stupid—the comedy comes from contemplating creatures inferior to us in perception and understanding. The clever animals are corrupt, and corrupt *because* they are clever. When Orwell tells us that Boxer is 'not of first-rate intelligence', the understatement is so massive as to be comic, for Boxer is the eternal simpleton asking to be cheated by the first trickster who happens along (p. 6). Boxer trusts others: that is at once his splendour and his flaw. Hence our ambivalent response, for, if the sheep are idiots, Boxer is a noble idiot; can we totally withhold admiration as he drives himself to exhaustion for what he regards as the common good? However deluded the altruism, can we deride, and still honour the injunction, stressed by St Paul and Marx alike, that everyone should give his all for the community?

Nevertheless, checking the impulse towards admiration, is a counter-imperative that makes us confront the worse than worthless nature of Boxer's self-sacrifice, for, in so blindly giving his great strength to a corrupt regime, he adds, however unintentionally, to the world's evil. As cruelly as in Ibsen, the very virtues of the foolish idealist make the world a worse place: heroism without insight abets corruption. 'Unnatural vices / Are fathered by our heroism.' Eliot's terrible paradox in 'Gerontion' is equally applicable to Boxer.

Immoral intelligence is a nightmare, virtue without wisdom is evil's unwitting accomplice, while an intelligence content to perceive but loath to amend the world is futile. Benjamin the donkey is plainly no fool; with Orwell's approval, he shreds the old theodicy argument. Told that God gave him a tail to keep off the flies, he replies that he would sooner have neither (*Animal Farm*, p. 6). It recalls Orwell's own wry remonstration when told how lucky he had been to be shot through the throat; he reflected that he would have been even luckier not to be shot at all (*Homage*, pp. 185–6). But in Benjamin's case the sharpness topples into cynicism. Though not himself a knave, he is reprehensibly ready to let the knaves have it all their own way, without even a struggle.

Orwell's was a very different temper and we cannot imagine him approving Benjamin's defeatism. 'It is better from the point of view of survival to fight and be conquered than to surrender without fighting' (*CEJL*, II, 302). So Orwell rebuked those who wished to sue for peace after the fall of France. When the situation worsened, he became correspondingly more bellicose: "If the USA is going to submit to conquest as well, there is nothing for it but to die fighting, but one must above all die *fighting* and have the satisfaction of killing someone else first' (II, 397). The Hollywood version of *Nineteen Eighty-Four* ends with Winston, in a heroic Alamo-style last stand, machine-gunning Big Brother's hordes as they attack in waves—certain to die, he is nevertheless unconquerable. This hero's death is precisely what Orwell, for his own despondent purposes, denies Winston in the novel.

Yet there is no doubt that Orwell prefers fighter to quitter; even Hitler is commended for saying that 'to accept defeat destroys the soul of a nation', and Orwell berates Burnham for his alacrity in bowing down to the latest conqueror (*CEJL*, II, 132; IV, 205–6). Defeat is, in a sense, unimportant, provided there is no capitulation. Early in the war, while arguing for an English socialist government, he declares that, even if it were beaten by the Nazis, 'its memory will be as dangerous to the victor, as the memory of the French Revolution was dangerous to Metternich's Europe' (II, 127). Orwell's combativeness decisively separates him from Benjamin. Boxer acts but never knows; Benjamin *knows*, but does not act; do nothing, he advises, for nothing is worth doing. Such quietism surrenders the world to those who can he trusted always to act for the worst. Orwell's is a completely different temperament. If, as he says, the first instinct of the writer is to shun politics, nevertheless 'it is not possible for any thinking person to live in such a society as our own without wanting to change it' (I, 374). Benjamin conspicuously fails the test.

For the first time, we have difficulty finding Orwell in his own book. Hitherto, the author is too obtrusive, the characters too often mouthpieces for his affirmations. *Animal Farm* is his most impersonal work, in which he comes closest to Stephen Dedalus's ideal of the authorial self refined out of existence, or to that power of negative capability identified by Keats as the mark of the chameleon poet equally elated at the creation of an Iachimo or an Imogen.

We can, of course, infer Orwell's anti-utopian temper from the difficulties that almost immediately challenge Old Major's dream and convict him as another of those 'speculatists' arraigned by Burke—difficulties that seem rooted in nature rather than in some social injustice that a return to nature will abolish. Even as Old Major rhapsodises over comradeship, the cat displays a selfish prudence by claiming the warmest place at the meeting and then purrs in selfish satisfaction throughout the speech without listening to a word. Meanwhile, Mollie exhibits an equally selfish folly by concentrating on ribbons and gewgaws while the momentous speech goes unregarded. Are these variants of selfishness the product of nature or nurture? Can we conceive, under different environmental conditions, a less flighty mare, an altruistic cat?

The question is crucial, since Major's speech drags the dilemma into the forefront of consciousness: is the unhappy life of the animals attributable to human mismanagement (Jones staggering off drunk to bed without feeding them) or 'is this simply part of the order of nature?' For Major the question is rhetorical: misery is man-made, nature neither explains nor justifies it. Yet his confidence stems surely from a simplistic and abbreviated view of what nature means. For him it signifies simply the external conditions: farm, farmer, soil, climate, and so on. The farm is fertile and could easily support an even greater number of animals at a far higher level of comfort and dignity. That it doesn't presently do so is the fault of the parasitical Jones, who consumes without producing, creaming off the profit while allowing the animals only enough to maintain the labour force. 'Man is the only real enemy we have' (p. 9). Eliminate the enemy and the gates of an animal Eden swing invitingly open.

Orwell guards against the siren simplicity of a single explanation by a much more inclusive definition of the word 'nature'. This must take account not only of external factors, such as the farm's fertility and the farmer's fecklessness, but also of the internal dispositions of the animals themselves: the mare's frivolity and the cat's selfishness, the horse's impercipience and the sheep's mindlessness, the donkey's defeatism and the pig's ambition. Orwell exposes thereby the revolutionary fallacy of a single foe whose liquidation will, at a stroke, transform the world into paradise, the Raskolnikov paralogism that only the pawnbroker thwarts happiness.

'Only get rid of Man', exhorts Old Major (p. 10), and then, by implication, it is clear walking to the just society: substitute kulaks or Jews or any other single group and we have the same pernicious psychology leading to the same atrocities. Not that Jones is innocent; he *is* drunken and irresponsible, has no cause to complain at expropriation. Unlike Burke lamenting the French king, Orwell is not soliciting sympathy for the displaced farmer, but warning the revolutionary people that toppling the tyrant initiates rather than solves the problem. The link, again, is with traditional Christianity. When the Pharisees reproached Jesus for carelessness towards ritual purity, he replied that the real corruption is internal. Far more important than the external differences between Jones and the animals are the ominous internal similarities: the shared irresponsibility, selfishness and rapacity, the threat to Utopia from within which will survive the ejection of Jones or the killing of the Romanovs. Not the human enemies massing at Foxwood, but the secret survival within the new community of those characteristics of greed and cruelty which the story demonstrates as *not* the monopoly of human beings— this is the real danger to Major's dream.

In Hawthorne's story *'Earth's Holocaust'*, which also records the elated initiation of another great utopian project, the founding of America, there is a similar caution against simplistic optimism. There, Europe is the rejected external evil, America the new immaculate conception whose purity is allegedly certified by the huge bonfire in which all the symbols of transcended European depravity are being burned. But, even while the new Adams of the reconstituted Eden rejoice, the devil laughs in the background confident that his imperium still stands, because the hearts of these fugitive Europeans, those foul rag-and-bone shops brought with them to the New World, are outside the purifying flames. 'O, take my word for it, it will be the old world yet!' Satan's exultant cry at the end of Hawthorne's story might serve as epigraph to *Animal Farm*.

Where *'Earth's Holocaust'* consigns crowns and mitres, charters and lawbooks to the fire, *Animal Farm* makes a bonfire of the bits and chains, knives and whips which testify to the oppression of animals at human hands.

In each case, the confident assumption is that the wrongdoing is gone for ever, that both America and Animal Farm are new worlds, sinless creations; in each case, too, is emphasised the futility of large-scale reforms that leave the heart untouched, for the unreformed heart will find a way of forging new chains long after the bonfire meant to rid the world of them has collapsed into ash. No more than the fall of the Bastille or the storming of the Winter Palace does the destruction of the harness room in itself guarantee the end of tyranny.

Utopia slights nature: everything is declared possible, with nature at worst a sluggish servant whom a sharp reprimand will bring to heel. Failure must accordingly be the result of neglect or malice. The windmill on the farm *cannot* have been blown down by a storm—that would be condemning nature as reactionary—so there must be treachery, betrayal, a criminal conspiracy, an evil genius, Trotsky, Goldstein, Snowball. Whenever anything miscarries on the farm, the pigs immediately blame Snowball or the rats or both. The totalitarian mentality cannot accommodate fallibility, only malevolence. Nor can there be genuine, rational disagreement, for disagreement is simply the strategy of malcontents—there is no case to make for Lucifer, for he is purely subversive. *All* disagreement indicates latent ill will, like the leper's scales, the sign of inner corruption. Truth is manifest, and those who resist it sin against the light.

Animal Farm depicts an attempt to exalt culture above nature: there are no natural disasters, simply human malevolence; no natural limits, for the will is arbiter of reality; no natural blessings, for, if the sun shines and the water tastes sweet, the credit is Napoleon's. One senses in Orwell a very different mentality, a conviction that politics can only go so far, that it is as absurd to praise the leader for every boon as to blame him for every hardship: 'there is a great deal of inherent sadness and loneliness in human life that would be the same whatever the external circumstances' (*CEJL*, IV, 480). Any animal asserting this would have found himself in trouble with Napoleon for defeatism and subversion.

Always in Orwell a sense of the real checks utopian aspiration. It soon becomes clear that the farm needs certain materials, such as iron for the horses' shoes, which can only be obtained from the abhorred human beings. In *Darkness at Noon* a similar dilemma drives Litle Loewy to kill himself. How is the new, redeemed society to live in the world, as it must, without being contaminated by it? Ye are a separate people, come from among them. Yet, however inspiring the idea of separateness may be when consciousness of rebirth is still intoxicatingly fresh, history indicates the extreme difficulty of maintaining such puritan zeal over long periods and among large numbers. Sooner or later the world invades the vision, compelling the visionaries to adjust or perish, extorting even from the inflexible some measure of compromise. Can there be compromise without betrayal? It is the same dilemma as faced the early Christians when the expected end of the world didn't occur and the sentiments of the Sermon on the Mount had to be adjusted to the requirements of an institutional church. *Animal Farm* enacts a similar jarring collision of Utopia and nature.

'Weak or strong, clever or simple, we are all brothers' (p. 12). Old Major's words might be straight out of one of those well-meaning thoroughly futile papal encyclicals that Orwell condemned as laughably irrelevant to real life. Fine words, but they proclaim as fact what is at best a prayer—and a prayer even further from realisation at the end of the book than when first uttered. All brothers? Sparrows and cats, dogs and rats? Can the lamb lie down *with* rather than *inside* the lion? *Animal Farm* shows that the only possible relationship between strong and weak, clever and simple, is that of exploiter to exploited. In fairness to Old Major, he does caution his freedom-fighters not to forget the threat from within: 'And remember also that in fighting against Man, we must not come to resemble him' (pp. 11–12). Nietzsche similarly admonishes us to avoid becoming the dragons we contend with, a caution which Orwell himself repeats (*CEJL*, III, 267).

Nevertheless, Old Major must take some responsibility for the gap between dream and reality, rhetoric and fact, that the book exploits. Even as he exhorts the animals to unite against the single enemy—'all men are enemies. All animals are comrades' (*Animal Farm*, p. 11)—the dogs suddenly attack the rats; reality shatters the myth of fraternity and exposes the blunder of promoting wish to fact. The lesson is lost, however, as Major calls for a vote on the question, 'Are rats comrades?', securing, predictably, a resounding affirmative—as though votes could abolish a natural enmity, or majorities, however overwhelming, alter reality. As well vote down the law of gravity or instruct wolves to turn herbivorous. True, only the three dogs and the cat refuse to accept rats as comrades, but an astute rat will take no comfort from hearing the sheep swear eternal friendship while his natural predators remain implacable as ever. Trusting to the sanctity of majority decisions in such a case must lead to a short career with a bloody conclusion. Democracy cannot overrule nature: an ineradicable hostility is exhibited at the very instant it is being so magniloquently repudiated.

'Jones will sell you to the knacker' (p. 10): doubtless only the rebellion prevents the prophecy from coming true. But, just as Brutus blundered in thinking to kill kingship with Caesar, so Major errs in assuming that Jones's expulsion means an end to exploitation. The spirit of Caesar triumphs in the play, and, equally, the spirit of Jones takes up fresh quarters in the new rulers of the farm. Boxer's destiny is the knacker because ingratitude and rapacity are not a human monopoly. The temptation to believe that evil can be expunged with the removal of one single enemy is for ever punished in those who succumb to it: new presbyter is but old priest writ large, today's freedom-fighter can so easily become tomorrow's tyrant, and the final shocking metamorphosis of *Animal Farm* leaves the exploited unable to distinguish pigs from men.

The fable presents alternatives as disturbingly unattractive as those of *Mansfield Park* or the 'Digression on Madness'. Jane Austen forces a choice between the dull, Houyhnhnm goodness of Fanny Price and the scandalous Yahoo vivacity of Mary Crawford, denying us the third option we desire, one that unites wit and virtue in one irresistible combination. *Mansfield Park* declines to supply a heroine who will gratify simultaneously our moral and aesthetic impulses. Where Jane Austen matches art against morality, Orwell pits decency against politics. 'What you get over and over again is a movement of the proletariat which is promptly canalised and betrayed by astute people at the top, and then the growth of a new governing class. The one thing that never arrives is equality . . . men are only decent when they are powerless' (*CEJL*, I, 372).

Power and decency simply will not set up house together; the brief ecstacy of revolutionary Barcelona simply confirms this pessimist conclusion, when the tragically short honeymoon ends in the old familiar divorce. All history is a history of elites, and the elite always employs its superior abilities to further its own interests. The reader of Orwell's fable is trapped with a choice he can neither make nor evade: stupid, altruistic horse, born for the knacker after a lifetime of exploitation, or clever, selfish pig, fulfilling the intellectual's dream of commandeering the whip—fool or knave, in the deliberately offensive terminology of Orwell's master, Swift. Within the text there is nowhere else to go if, disliking both alternatives, we decline to fall in behind Napoleon or Boxer: to avoid the knacker, must we wield the whip? The bridgeless chasm between power and righteousness postulated by *Animal Farm* supplies the agonising answer.

Benjamin is no help; though eluding the dualism of corrupt power and fatuous innocence, he leaves the dilemma intractable as ever. He sees what is happening but does nothing to change it; the one dubious benefit of his intelligence is that *he* will not go to the knacker in deluded fidelity—but he *will* go nevertheless. His attitude might just escape condemnation within a framework of belief that demotes this life in favour of the life to come—let the Napoleons enjoy their brittle triumphs while they heap up damnation to themselves—but neither Benjamin nor Orwell believes any such thing. Orwell is not endorsing Benjamin's cynical *ataraxia*, his indifference to, even amusement at the surrounding perfidy. Hence the curious blend of delight and unease provoked in us by the book, for within it there is no one figure or viewpoint claiming our unreserved allegiance. The segregation of qualities is deliberately disturbing, for we do not want to be Napoleon or Boxer or Benjamin, rather to take from each what is valuable while repudiating his particular defects—to be energetic, forceful, intelligent, shrewd, wary, heroic and virtuous all at once.

Yet things begin so promisingly. The early revolutionary days are a farmyard evocation of egalitarian Barcelona. Snowball's appeal to gather the harvest more quickly than under the former dispensation is nobly answered; the animals are asked to work harder as 'a point of honour', and the result is an increased harvest, with not even, as in pre-revolutionary days, a single case of theft. 'Everyone worked according to his capacity . . . nobody stole, nobody grumbled over his rations, the quarrelling and biting and jealousy which had been normally features of life in the old days had almost disappeared' (*Animal Farm*, p. 27). The old Adam seems overcome, the miracle of a reconsecrated nature apparently accomplished. Orwell at this point means to show the failure of revolution as a betrayal, a crime of leadership; the animals as a whole transcend their natures only to be let down by unworthy guides. 'Not an animal on the farm had stolen so much as a mouthful' (p. 26); meanwhile the pigs are grabbing milk and apples for themselves. The animals dream of comradeship and self-government all the while they are being duped. Boxer, a Hercules of altruism, is cynically exploited as a noble simpleton. The inference is that, given a leadership worthy of its followers, the revolutionary miracle might be achieved.

Yet, even already, ominous signs of the limits set to revolution by nature are visible. 'The behaviour of the cat was somehow peculiar' (p. 27): this is how the narrator describes the scrounging cat, always eager to eat, never present to work. *Is* selfishness really so exceptional, Boxer's noble self-disregard so routine? Isn't there something impertinent in the easy assumption that men are generous as oranges are sweet? That the cat isn't really so extraordinary becomes increasingly clear as the book proceeds to heighten the discrepancy between nature and theory, shows, indeed, how revolution can be pushed to such an anti-natural extent that it becomes a species of folly. The clue is once again in Swift, this time in the Academy of Lagado. Two very different kinds of folly are exhibited there: first, that which seeks to extract sunshine from cucumbers, breed sheep without wool, and similar lunacies; second, and even more idiotic, that which dreams of founding a just polity with good laws and honest rulers. Orwell borrows from Lagado in making his own analysis of farmyard follies. The Clean Tails League for the Cows, the Whiter Wool Movement for the Sheep, the Wild Comrades' Re-education Committee (to tame rats and rabbits) are all on a par with the zanier Lagado projects, and meet, of course, the same fate. 'The attempt to tame the wild creatures . . . broke down almost immediately. They continued to behave very much as before, and, when treated with generosity, simply took advantage of it' (p. 29). There are limits as to how far nature can be re-educated or reality restructured. Only the cat remains zealous for re-education, renouncing her customary indolence to join its committee, for ever persuading the sparrows to perch on her paw now that all animals are comrades—'but the sparows kept their distance' (ibid.). Boxer should have gone to school with such sensible sparrows, who wisely prefer harsh realism to delectable theory.

A key theme in Orwell's later work, from *Homage to Catalonia* onwards, is the power of words to alter reality, and Squealer is an expert at turning black into white. Yet even his skill doesn't excuse Boxer's credulity. Even Boxer cannot accept that the newly discredited Snowball has always been the secret accomplice of Jones, cannot forget the Battle of the Cowshed and the ocular proofs of Snowball's heroism. For a moment it seems as if experience will finally defeat dogma, reality take revenge on fideism. But Boxer's belief in Napoleon proves greater than an Alps of contrary evidence—if experience contradicts Napoleon, so much the worse for experience. Even when the dogs attack Boxer—and everyone knows that they never act save at Napoleon's command—the victorious horse, hoof poised above their throats, still looks to Napoleon for instructions, clinching proof of how suicidally credulous he is. Even after the traumatic shock of the executions, when, for the first time since Jones, animals are again killed, in punishment and by their own fellows, Boxer's faith still overcomes the facts: 'It must be due to some fault in ourselves' (*Animal Farm*, p. 75). *Credo quia impossibile est.* His solution is 'to work harder', to embrace work as the styptic to thought, the drug that will stupefy him as it stupefied Dorothy Hare, stifling the unbearable questions.

'A society of animals set free from hunger and the whip, all equal, each working according to his capacity, the strong protecting the weak' (pp. 75–6): only the corrupt will sneer at the ideal, only the exploiters desire its shipwreck. Yet the book shows the noble ideal to be as irrelevant as any pious encyclical exhorting the rich to love the poor—is it any less visionary to ask the clever to love the foolish? *Animal Farm* follows Gulliver to the citadel of delusion in the Academy of Lagado, the school of political projectors who seem to him 'wholly out of their senses' in a way far more blatant than the zany experiments he has just seen. These political enthusiasts dream of a just society where rulers serve their subjects' interests and officials are chosen on merit and rewarded for integrity, 'with many other wild impossible chimaeras, that never entered before into the heart of man to conceive' (p. 232). Compared to this, the sunbeam-extractors are hard-headed realists, the naked-sheep breeders the most practical of men. This is Boxer's folly: in killing himself for an animal paradise which becomes more remote the harder he strives, Boxer is attempting something that makes the Wild Comrades Re-education Movement seem child's-play.

Despite Clover's warnings against overtaxing himself, 'Boxer would never listen to her' (p. 55). Many centuries before Orwell wrote, Ecclesiastes supplied the epitaph to the horse's futile existence: 'He who quarries stones is hurt by them.' Yet simply to dismiss him as a fool is too much like becoming a spokesman for Jones and the reactionary Iagos who delight in human failure and folly. The problem once again springs from the book's unpalatable alternatives. The constant cry of the pigs is that the choice is Jones or them, and that to criticize them is in effect to recall him. It is a winner because among the animals it is axiomatic that there should be no return to Jones. On the other hand a reading of the text seems to lend credence to the argument of the Joneses that to overthrow them is to establish pig rule, and nobody wants that either.

The reader must make the necessary discriminations. The aim is to end exploitation, not replace capitalist incompetents by soviet pigs, to transcend both Jones and Napoleon, just as Orwell had insisted that Hitler must be defeated in order to surpass both Churchill and Stalin, not to reinforce either imperialism. The problem is even graver than the fact that this desired resolution is not within the book; far worse is the book's implicit argument that only a miraculous psychological transformation can make such a resolution possible. 'Without education of the masses, no social progress; without social progress, no education of the masses' (*CEJL*, II, 279). The pessimistic impasse he found in Koestler is equally discernible in his own book.

The horses' virtues are disconcertingly yoked to their inadequacies: unable to think for themselves, they need leaders, and their fidelity is inseparable from stupidity. These leaders are 'the most intelligent animals', for, in the awakening of consciousness that follows Major's speech, 'the work of teaching and organizing fell *naturally* upon the pigs' (*Animal Farm*, p. 15). The adverb is crucial; but, if nature initially seems the solution to the problem of liberation, it soon presents itself as its most intractable component. The backward animals need leaders, but, since leader means exploiter, freedom remains elusive as ever. Nature, making the pigs clever, simultaneously makes them selfish; good is stupid, clever bad, and the result is impasse. Eliot's trust in elitism blinds him to this aspect of Orwell's fable. Eliot rejected the manuscript not because it was offensive to Stalin, but because it was, in his view, unfair to the pigs. As the most intelligent animals, they were necessarily best qualified to run the farm; what was needed, according to

Eliot, was not more communism but more public-spirited pigs. Within the terms of *Animal Farm* this is about as sensible as asking for god-fearing atheists.

Orwell inherits from Swift a distrust of intelligence without integrity; there is no greater danger than a clever rogue. Jones's overthrow poses a whole series of unprecedented problems for the new regime, but the pigs are so resourceful that solutions come easily. The pigs are a meritocracy of aptitude, a natural elite: 'with their superior knowledge, it was natural that they should assume the leadership' (p. 25). What could be more natural than for those who know to lead those who don't? Just as naturally, the pigs don't work—their task is to organise and supervise. Hierarchy is the law of nature. Equally natural is the compulsion of elites to pursue their own advantage against every other consideration. Egoism is implicit in leadership from the beginning. Snowball and Napoleon quarrel over everything because nothing matters but the power struggle—who gives the orders, not what the orders are.

The skill of reading is made revelatory of this potential for corruption. There is a contradition in the fact that activities such as reading and writing, so incontestably part of the tainted past, should be retained and cultivated in the purified polity. Boxer's touchingly naïve idealism, his readiness to be faithful at the cost of his own comfort, is revealed when, obedient to Snowball's Savonarola-like command that all clothes are human, hence evil, he burns the straw hat which protects him against flies. But if everything human is corrupt, as Old Major teaches, why are the most intelligent animals cultivating these depraved arts from the outset? Snowball plans the Battle of the Cowshed by studying Caesar's Gallic wars, scrutinises *The Farmer and Stockbreeder* to improve his knowledge of agrarian reform. The reading-skills of the animals become an infallible index of their characters and dispositions: the pigs are excellent, the dogs very good, as befits the leading echelons of the new elite, while Boxer, try as he will, can never master more than a few letters of the alphabet. Benjamin can read but won't, because he says there is nothing worth reading; Mollie, in learning only the letters that form her name, betrays the narcissism that is her defining characteristic. Reading is the Rorschach test that is unerringly diagnostic of character: how you read determines who you are.

The pigs, claiming the milk and apples for themselves, simply prove that good readers make good swindlers, with the intellect a yes-man to appetite, a means to justify theft and selfishness. "The animals had assumed as a matter of course that these [the apple windfalls] I would be shared out equally' (p. 32). The assumption reveals an enslavement to dogma, an inability to think against the grain of cherished preconceptions. If only men are exploiters, their overthrow must end exploitation, and the apples must be equally divided. Even when this doesn't happen, dogma continues to over-rule experience. If Jones keeps the apples, the act is by definition exploita-tion; but animals cannot exploit, so, even if the pigs act like Jones, it must be for the common good. Under Jones the animals used to get some of the milk, now all of it is appropriated by the pigs as one of the perquisites of command. 'We pigs are brain-workers', claims Squealer—and brain-workers must have milk and apples to function aright (ibid.).

Squealer even argues that the pigs take apples from a sense of duty rather than a taste for fruit, almost in a spirit of self-sacrifice, because science has proved apples essential to the well-being of pigs. 'Do not imagine, comrade, that leadership is a pleasure!' (p. 50). Squealer's success in presenting leadership as an irksome duty, nobly undertaken from pure phil-anthropy, leaves the animals helpless in face of the pigs' arrogation of privi-leges. This idea of the elite as an ascetic, altruistic group, whose powers and privileges are, properly understood, modes of self-deprivation, can be traced back to Plato and is at the heart of the Grand Inquisitor's impassioned denunciation of Christ. When Napoleon ludicrously poses as society's martyr, it is simply an outrageously comic version of the same specious argu-ment advanced by Mann's protagonist in *Mario and the Magician*. Whether it be milk and apples, beds and blankets, whatever extra privilege is claimed or law set aside, the underlying argument is the same: the pigs need this to be efficient, and the state needs the pigs to survive; always, too, is the same underlying threat—to question pig privileges is to connive at Jones's return. His reaction to the hands-off-Russia argument shows how irritated Orwell could become at such pig logic: 'if . . . you express a mild distaste for slave-labour camps or one-candidate elections, you are either insane or actu-ated by the worst motives' (*CEJL*, IV, 454); Orwell inverts the argument: for him, *not* to criticize the pigs is to betray the revolution.

And yet it must be noted that never once throughout the fable does Orwell side with the human beings against the animals. It is one more crucial differentiation between himself and Benjamin. The donkey watches in amusement as the invaders place the dynamite in the mill, disdainfully aloof from the dispute and contemptuous of his fellow animals, Napoleon included, who fail to see the significance of what is happening (*Animal Farm*, p. 88). Orwell eschews such detachment, cannot so easily smile at the tragic devastation of animal hopes and efforts. The hysterical abuse launched by the human beings against Animal Farm, the wild charges of cannibalism, of females held in common, and so on, recall right-wing abuse of Republican Spain. So opposed to this is Orwell that he deliberately breaks the parallel with Russia by not having the animals harm, far less eat, their human oppressors—there is no similarity between the fates of the

Joneses and the Romanovs; and where could one find a more decently traditional marriage than that between Boxer and Clover?

The reason for Orwell's opposition to the human beings is perfectly
plain: they *want* the farm to fail, detest the tale of its prosperity, fume at the
revolutionary hymn, 'Beasts of England', sneering at it as rubbish, yet flog-
ging the singers on their own farms. Orwell's style alone is enough to reveal
a very different outlook: 'And yet the song was irrepressible. The blackbirds
whistled it in the hedges, the pigeons cooed it in the elms, it got into the din
of the smithies and the tune of the church bells' (p. 36). The style is as buoy-
antly irrepressible as the song itself, recalling Dicken's zestful description of
the playful wind that blows us into *Martin Chuzzlewit*. The song not merely
captures animal nature (blackbirds, pigeons), something totally consonant
with the fable's datum, but, less predictably, reverberates in both man's
honest labour and ancestral piety (anvils and church bells). Such a song is
irresistibly destined to fill the world, for all that is good in life echoes it, and
only what is shamefully selfish stays dumb.

When the style modulates from lively joy to sonorous dignity, to the
vaticidal rhetoric of *The Communist Manifesto*, Orwell's antipathy to selfish
humanity is made more manifest: 'And when the human beings listened to it
[the hymn], they secretly trembled, hearing in it a prophecy of their future
doom' (*Animal Farm*, p. 36). Wherever in the fable man means exploiter (the
smith in the context clearly isn't), Orwell sides unreservedly with the rebels.
In the last quotation the farmyard is momentarily transcended, the petty
altercations raised to a new cleave of being, as astonishing as though
Lilliputian vanities were suddenly to claim unironic attention. The distance
enjoyed by the reader in virtue of the Aesopian form temporarily disappears
to make him participant rather than amused Olympian.

Serious or comic, there is no question that Orwell consistently
opposes the human beings. Orwell detected in Gulliver's description of
how the Houyhnhnms would rout an invading English army evidence of
Swift's 'quislingism', his unpatriotic longing to see Marlborough's troops
humiliated by any foe, even if it meant horses succeeding where the French
had failed (*CEJL*, IV, 244). What might Swift have retorted after contemplating the 'terrifying spectacle' of Boxer in the battle against the human
invaders of Animal Farm? Orwell is as unequivocally partisan for the animals
as Swift for the Houynhnhnms, though he lacks the master's ferocity; no one
can miss the relish in Swift's account of the would-be colonisers battered to
mummy by the horses' terrible hooves—Orwell, by contrast, is content to
see the men merely routed rather than trampled to death.

Still, his enmity to the human beings is unmistakable and constant, so
much so that, repudiating their anti-animal propaganda, he occasionally

forgets the moral of his own fable. He tells us that humans 'against their will
. . . had developed a certain respect for the efficiency with which the animals
were managing their own affairs' (*Animal Farm*, p. 58). Yet, as his story shows,
the animals are *not* managing their own affairs; a pig oligarchy rules, with the
other animals as cruelly exploited as ever. Only internally will Orwell attack
the new society; let an outsider hint the same criticism and he at once
becomes the farm's champion, almost as though he has personally espoused
the resolution of the new anthem: 'Animal Farm, Animal Farm, never
through me will you come to harm.' Motive is the decisive consideration.
Those who criticise the farm in the hope of eradicating its defects should be
heeded, whereas those who parade these defects with malicious glee and a
craving for the farm's collapse must be exposed as the hypocrites they are.

The description of how 'the cowardly enemy' break and flee at the
successful animal counterattack is illuminating, for this is Orwell's adjec-
tive, not Squealer's (p. 89). Similarly revealing is the passage describing
how the animals indomitably gather to rebuild the demolished windmill
against the concentrated ill will of 'the envious human beings' (p. 64).
When was Iago ever a model or envy ever an admirable quality? Realism
may sometimes command our allegiance, envy never. The sensible man
who warns against extravagant aspiration should be heard, but the sneerer,
with a vested interest in the spirit's humiliation, eager that every hope
should miscarry and avid for abortion, is a noisome pest and a spreader of
pollution. The deluded Othello is tricked into believing his wife the whore
that Iago resents her not being, but there is a world of difference between
the man who laments the pity of it and him who rejoices to find virtue a
cheat, or, worse still, strives to make it so.

Hence Orwell's complaint at Rayner Heppenstall's radio version of
Animal Farm that it cast 'a sop to those stinking Catholics'—those same
bigoted reactionaries who almost worked the miracle of making Orwell
sympathise even with Stalin. Orwell had no intention of defending the *status
quo* of Western social injustice or of supplying ammunition to those whom
he had always regarded as enemies. If the Tories were unacceptable as 'the
stupid party', they were doubly so when they grew intelligent, for then, so
Orwell cautioned, it was time to feel for your watch and count your small
change (*CEJL*, III, 316). Orwell confronts the utopian shipwreck with
sadness, not with the *Schadenfreude* of the reactionary Iagos who would be
chagrined to see it sail home. It is all the more ironical, then, that this book,
which caused him the greatest sweat and gave him the greatest pleasure,
which brought him international fame and financial independence, should
have been acclaimed by simplistically anti-revolutionary groups in a spirit
contrary to everything he stood for.

Orwell despises liars, whatever their political complexion, whether shedding crocodile tears over the failure of the great experiment or cynically coining the revolutionary ideals to their own selfish advantage. He doesn't like the envious human beings who want the farm to fail, but neither does he approve the fatuous fellow travellers who visit the farm, see only what the pigs permit, and return home to regurgitate the lies they have swallowed. The noble attempt to build the just society is good, despite human propaganda against, and, more damaging still, Squealer's propaganda for it. It is because Orwell believes in the ethos of service and the dignity of labour that he finds the sentiments unforgivably offensive in Squealer's mouth, much as for Chaucer the sacred topics of grace and redemption are polluted in the Pardoner's patter. What a man says must be assessed in the light of his motive, for the speaker thereby condemns himself rather than the high ideals he traduces—not to see this is to line up with the pig and the Pardoner.

Since the pigs are liars, Orwell opposes them whatever they say. Boxer thinks Napoleon is always right; Orwell shows him as always wrong. The new anthem celebrates Napoleon as 'Lord of the swill-bucket', guarantor of 'full belly twice a day, clean straw to roll upon', and the context makes it clear that Orwell despises this as squalid materialism, the trough philosophy castigated by Carlyle (*Animal Farm*, p. 80). Yet Orwell favoured full bellies, and the human equivalent of clean straw, never ceased to denounce the deprivations of the poor. His first concern was to improve the material lot of the people and he stipulated this as a necessary condition of future progress—necessary, though not sufficient. There must be more to life than a full belly and a decent bed, and Orwell could even envisage situations where these good things could be used to subvert human dignity. The Salvation Army and Sweden struck him in this light, and to these we can unhesitatingly add Napoleon's Epicurean programme.

Later, however when another swing of the ideological seesaw exalts asceticism, Orwell is implacable as ever towards Napoleon. Now 'luxuries' are denounced as contrary to the spirit of Animalism; Snowball's dream of electrification and 'consumerism' is vilified as shamefully sybaritic—true happiness requires hard work and frugal living (p. 109). Orwell admired self-discipline and practiced it in his own life; but, conscious of the tainted source from which the present puritanical exhortations come, he is even more disgusted by the hypocrisy than by the former blatant appeal to the appetites. Whether endorsing Epicureanism or asceticism, Napoleon is always wrong because his motive is always corrupt.

It is because Orwell opposes exploiters rather than men, cheats rather than capitalists, that his fable is even more relevant today than when first written. Now that the whites are going out all over Africa and the old colonialist exploiters have been displaced, the new native rulers have often proved to be no better than the expelled foreigners, and paradise remains remote as ever.

> The hand of Vengeance found the Bed
> To which the Purple Tyrant fled;
> The iron hand crush'd the Tyrant's head
> And became a Tyrant in his stead.

Blake's lines are still sharply pertinent. Orwell's perception that wickedness comes from the heart and not from the peculiar doctrines of particular groups signifies his manumission from ideology. Just as Kostoglotov, reading the explanation for the empty cage in the zoo, experiences relief at the breaking of the ideological cage, so, too, *Animal Farm* exhibits a similar simplicity in recording the victory of ethics over politics, a similar insistence on honesty regardless of partisan advantage. The pity is that so many of its readers, in using it to make political capital, are incapable of matching the honesty of Orwell's text.

Nowhere is the honesty more impressive, nowhere is he more indisputably Swift's pupil than at the book's climax, that moment of stunning metamorphosis when the pigs visibly become the exploiters they have sought to be since the idea of revolution was born. Only human beings are exploiters: so unchallengeable is Old Major's dogma, so unshakable the axiom of animal innocence, that exploiters must take human form before the oppressed can recognize them. Mr Pilkington, by contrast, doesn't allow mere externals to obscure community of interest: 'was not the labour problem the same everywhere?' he rhetorically asks his pig hosts (*Animal Farm*, pp. 117–18). From his standpoint Animal Farm is a thoroughly admirable society, and his praise in itself proves that the model workers' republic has become a model of exploited labour, with its lower animals duplicating his lower classes.

Yet, the long series of swindles notwithstanding, the gullible animals go on trusting to appearances. No matter what the pigs *do*, they are still visibly animal, hence, by irrefutable dogma, comrades. The animals continue throughout prisoners of ideology, shackled to *a priori* preconceptions despite the empirical contradictions, intoning that four legs means friend and two enemy, in disregard of the fact that a lamb would be safer with St Francis than with a wolf. Not until the shocking anagnorisis, when the pigs become in form what they have long been in substance, do the dogmatic scales fall from the animals' eyes, and, finally escaping these parade-ground categorisations, they see themselves as they truly are: not a band of brothers, each contributing according to his ability and receiving according to his needs, but a class society, no different from any other exploited workforce on any other farm. It is a sickening admission to make, and it should not surprise us that many still refuse to make it. 'For that day we must all labour'; 'some day it was coming': the strength of the aspiration is demonstrated in the perseverance of the pursuit—what, one wonders, does it take to extinguish the hopes raised by the October Revolution? In any case, Animal Farm is not the last, best hope of animalkind, the version of the future that works, but merely another depressing repetition of the old swindle, and its rechristening as Manor Farm, its ancient, pre-revolutionary title, simply acknowledges the fact. Yet facts can sometimes be so difficult to accept.

Never trust the teller, trust the tale. Lawrence's maxim has been endorsed by most modern critics as the only way to accord a text the proper respect. It is the more salutary in that biography has an arrogant habit of ordering the text what to say—if we know who a man is, then we can predict in advance, before turning a page, what his book must mean. Swift was a good Anglican clergyman, so how could his satires be anything other than a defence of Christianity? It follows, *a fortiori*, that Part Four of the *Travels*, for example, cannot possibly exhibit a pessimism inappropriate to an Anglican pulpit—if we find such pessimism, it's because we ourselves have planted it. We have misread the book, and the unopposable proof of this misreading is that our exegesis will not square with the datum of the Anglican Dean which is the indispensable precondition for any valid reading: *don't* trust the tale until after you've had a good look at the teller.

Something similar to this is discernible in certain reactions to Orwell's last two books. Animal Farm is manifestly an attack on Stalinism, but those on the right who gleefully embraced it somehow contrived to miss that it is just as palpably an attack on capitalism. Mr Pilkington is no better than Napoleon—that's the point of the climactic confusion when the bewildered animals can no longer tell one from the other. Orwell did not expose the Soviets to make the world safe for General Motors. The temptation then, is to insist that the book attacks Stalinism but not revolution, that, in exposing the *betrayal* of revolution, it leaves the concept itself inviolate. That, after all, is what we would expect from a fervent democratic socialist who had already shown that he was fully prepared to use force to overthrow otherwise irremovable tyrants. How could *Animal Farm* be against revolution? Such a conclusion would be in outrageously impermissable contradiction to everything we know about the man who wrote it.

And yet there is that awkward text; even those indignant at the alleged perversion of its meaning exhibit a kind of embarrassment as they try to explain away what for them are its indiscretions. Here, too, the example of Swift is instructive as we recall him trying to muffle the scandal of *The Tale of a Tub* by insisting that it was a *defence* of true religion and simply an exposé of certain religious aberrations. Not many of those who have read the text, then or since, have been persuaded. We are told of *Animal Farm* that 'it can be read as a lament for the fate of revolutions', but the very tone of the concession makes it plain that it would be a mistake to do so. Another critic reluctantly admits that 'no doubt *Animal Farm* can be taken as a book preaching that "all revolutions are failures"', but again the implicit warning is unmistakable: what can and what ought to be done are two very different things. Sensible men refrain from doing many things that they can do, and sensible readers of *Animal Farm* will reject interpretations, however possible, that clash violently with our prior image of Orwell as man. Orwell abhorred Stalin and personally took up arms to fight for a better society. It follows that *Animal Farm* attacks Stalin but not revolution; it records a failure, but 'the point is . . . that we must be clear as to what causes the failure'. Since Orwell's love for the simple animals is clear from the opening page, he must be attributing this failure to the wickedness of the leaders; the pigs are completely to blame, Stalin and the Politburo betrayed the Russian Revolution. So runs the argument.

It is, however, an argument heroically, fideistically maintained against the evidence *in* the text; Orwell's life becomes a sort of drill sergeant ordering the text to perform all sorts of manoeuvres at odds with its natural movement. For the fact is that *Animal Farm* does depict the failure of revolution, that, regardless of what Orwell did or believed *outside* its pages, *within* them he bravely endures the disintegration of the beliefs of a lifetime—its heroism is inseparable from the heresy which he enjoins upon the writer as his prime duty (*CEJL*, IV, 468). Does anyone really believe that when Orwell recommended heresy he meant it only for other people? The fearful heresy contemplated by *Animal Farm* is that revolution must end in tyranny, and when we honestly investigate 'what causes the failure' we shall have to abandon, however reluctantly, any such simplistic explanation as the selfishness of the pigs. The pigs are certainly selfish, but the shortcomings of *all* the animals contribute to the tragedy. Not ideology but nature is at the root of the debacle—the power drives of some, the credulity of others, folly, cynicism and sheeplike conformity. A society without pigs, i.e. exploiters, is inconceivable; add to this Orwell's despairing conviction that the pigs, thanks to their superior intelligence, will always manage to become the leaders, and it is plain that we have moved beyond a record of the historical betrayal of *one* revolution to an analysis of betrayal as a pathology intrinsic to *all* revolutions. That is what makes the book a classic and endows it with a quality of universality, transcending the historical occasion that provoked it. Stalin and

Napoleon are replaceable variables in an essentially determined process; Trotsky and Snowball would doubtless have developed other variations of perfidy, but the Revolution would have failed just the same. That is what *Animal Farm* says; we need not like it or agree, but neither should we suppress it in favour of what we would prefer it to say or think it ought to be saying. Orthodoxy, with Old Major as spokesman, insists that only man is the enemy; *Animal Farm* heretically demonstrates that, even if every human being disappeared, dogs would still hunt rats and cats stalk birds. The real, irremediable antagonisms are in nature rather than class—exploiter and exploited are irreducible categories that will not fade away, however much we transform politico-economic institutions. The text affirms this despite the fact that the author dedicated his life to transforming these very institutions. Empson's reminder that the text, especially when it is an allegory, has a life of its own with a separate and independent meaning, is certainly relevant— perhaps the metaphor of *Animal Farm* dictates the shape of the story, regardless of the writer's intention (*Life*, pp. 340, 362, 384, 397). But this takes away from the heroism of the book which is that it nerves itself to imagine a prospect that drains the meaning from Orwell's whole life's work. *Animal Farm* and *Nineteen Eighty-Four* are authenticated by the fact that their creator did not want them to be true.

Nevertheless, the form of the fable reprieves the reader from the sense of chill disillusion he must otherwise surely feel—we need only contrast it with its successor to see the truth of this. Moving from *Animal Farm* to *Nineteen Eighty-Four* is like leaving Lilliput for Brobdingnag, passing from a situation of control to one of helplessness: Gulliver the man mountain is shockingly reduced to the most impotent of creatures. *Animal Farm* diminishes, *Nineteen Eighty-Four* magnifies, and, while the diminution is a delight, the magnification is a nightmare. In the fable Stalin becomes Napoleon, and, however fearful on the farm, Napoleon cannot terrify us; like Jack at the end of *Lord of the Flies*, he dwindles in the presence of the adult human being, becomes, at worst, an unpleasant nuisance, never, what he is for his fellows, lord of life and death. However successful against the men in the fable, we know he could never take the farm away from *us*. In the prophecy Stalin becomes Big Brother, the tyrant in the most teleologically perfect sense, invincible, undeceivable, inescapable, god rather than man.

When Europe dwindles to a farm and twentieth-century history to a record of barnyard chicaneries, the effect is similar to that achieved by Swift when he presents the history of *his* times as the squabbles of Big- and Little-Endians, the rivalries of low heels and high. Becoming smaller, things become less menacing and more manageable. By contrast, the institutions and rulers of *Nineteen Eighty-Four* are monstrously and appallingly enlarged.

The whole world is dominated by three super-powers, and even Big Brother's acolyte, O'Brien, seems to the helpless Winston a kind of superman. The diminution is done to *us*, for it is Winston, the individual, the human representative, our spokesman, the last man in Europe, who shrivels into insignificance and, beyond that, to unpersonhood. On the farm the reader is like Swift in Lilliput, surveying, whether with amusement or exasperation, the antics of inferior beings, men and animals alike: we are not *in* but *above* the story, and it is this Olympian security that finally makes it a comedy in Aristotle's sense. But, in the dystopia, the reader, as entrapped as Gulliver in Brobdingnag, is made painfully aware through Winston of their shared nullity, and, in his enforced identification with the ruined 'hero', feels as impotent as Gulliver in the hands of the giants. Orwell's readers should fear the worst when he invites them to leave today's farm and accompany him on a journey to tomorrow's nightmare.

ROBERT SOLOMON

Ant Farm: An Orwellian Allegory

I'm not an Orwell scholar, and won't pretend to be. I'm not a political scientist, or a literary critic. I'm a philosopher, which might mean something very different to many of my colleagues, but, to me, it means being an anti-specialist, a writer whose discipline is dilettantism. Philosophers entertain theories and entertain thoughtful people with theories—the more abstract and unusual, perhaps, the better. In a symposium on George Orwell and *Nineteen Eighty-Four*, therefore, being a philosopher puts one at a certain disadvantage.

George Orwell was not at all abstract; indeed his few lapses into abstraction inevitably tended to be paradoxical, not unlike the willfully insidious paradoxes that emerge in *Nineteen Eighty-Four* and *Animal Farm*. He was a curiously heroic, pathetic, remarkably moral human being who sincerely believed that the salvation of the world was to be found only in, as he put it, "individual values," precisely those values—staunch if not heroic—that were so despairingly absent from *Nineteen Eighty-Four*. He believed himself to be, paradoxically, a man of principle who was not subservient to principles. Like many Enlightenment thinkers—and that, I believe, is what he was—he disdained abstraction and theory. He believed instead in the virtues, moral and intellectual. Class preferences aside, I would compare him most of all to Voltaire.

From *Reflections on America, 1984: An Orwellian Symposium.* © 1986 by the University of Georgia Press.

Orwell had an enormous impact when we read *Animal Farm* and *Nineteen Eighty-Four* during the previous cold war. Like most of my peers, I dreaded the coming of the year 1984 as the prophesied apocalypse; I never could think of that number as a mere literary device ("84" as an inversion of "48"). The current question, Have we made it to, if not yet through, 1984?, gets mixed answers. Some say, with a hint of hidden disappointment, "Yes, we have." Others have said, with a sense of relief, "No—things are just as bad as Orwell predicted they'd be. In fact worse, because we don't know they are so bad."

In between those rather dramatic extremes, of course, there were the dozen unrepeatable because simply tedious responses: "In some ways yes, in some ways no," and "Not us, but look at Russia and Chile," and "Wait until 1994." It is as if the very number—1984—precludes any response other than qualified gloom.

What do I think? I think that Orwell got it wrong, at least as prophecy. Some of it is a question of temperament. At least some of it is the unredeemed pessimism of a dying man, saying goodbye to a world he never did find very hospitable. But I think some of his error is, he would hate to hear, philosophical. I believe that he misunderstood the scope and variability of totalitarianism, much like Hannah Arendt, who was writing about the subject at the same time. And, I think that, more than Arendt, a philosopher (and a woman), his view of the world was too dark, too angry, too resentful, if not downright cranky. 1 984 may not be a good year for civil liberties or enlightenment, but it is hardly the overture to the apocalypse.

More philosophically, I have great trouble coming to grips with the admittedly attractive contrast between "individual values" and totalitarianism that permeates so much of his political writing and, of course, defines *Nineteen Eighty-Four*. It is a dichotomy that is too easy—and false. There are no individual values, in that sense. There are only shared values, including the mores, the morals, and the ideology (or ideologies) of a culture. Perhaps—but just perhaps—there are universal human values too. But Orwell, like Voltaire, was too suspicious, too hostile to ideas, as if all ideology were nothing but falsification and subterfuge. The positive role of ideas gets left out, and some other critical ingredients of culture and morality as well. It is worth noting once again that Orwell never felt as if he *belonged* anywhere. His indisputably enlightened moral opinions—and I do not say that sarcastically—share the enigmas of all Enlightenment views—detachment, resentment, and sometimes insidious philosophical perplexity about human nature, its differences and identities—his love of English breakfasts and the impossibility of communication in Burma notwithstanding. It is not surprising that Orwell, like Voltaire before and E. B. White after him, created his most powerful work by casting animals as his ideological spokescreatures and characters.

For all of its horrors, I find the world still more amusing than Orwell did or could. In a symposium on *Nineteen Eighty-Four*, however, I am afraid that the amusement in politics—the human circus—tends to be forgotten. I shall try to correct that here, and so turn to *Animal Farm*, not *Nineteen Eighty-Four*, which is relentlessly unamusing (not that *Animal Farm* has many light lines).

Orwell's concern in *Animal Farm* is not just Russia, of course. However exactly the plot and characters of the book may follow the Russian revolution from 1917 to 1943, the book far transcends that as an allegory and as a morality tale. It is a book about gullibility, manipulation, hypocrisy, and deception. My thesis—if I have one—is that these issues are more intricate than vigilante paranoia makes them seem. Orwell objected when *Time* magazine tried to use *Nineteen Eighty-Four* as cold-war propaganda; we can assume that he would be similarly indignant about the use to which his books have been put in this past year. The threat of totalitarianism is not limited to countries of Communist or "classical" totalitarian persuasion. In fact, one of the questions that has come more and more to disturb me in my philosophical reflections is the inherent dangers in the liberal Enlightenment tradition, and its defenses as well. The political and psychological dimensions of these dangers have been and will be discussed by the other symposium contributors. I would like to toy, in a manner that I hope is befitting to Orwell, with certain philosophical perplexities: the vocation and the isolation of intellectuals in America; the continual Enlightenment blindness to history which in *Nineteen Eighty-Four*, at least, required an elaborate set of deceptions from the top; the obsession with a paradoxical and extremely ill-defined concept of "freedom"; and what Philip Slater has often attacked as the simply ridiculous sense of individual uniqueness that is the heart of one brand of contemporary liberalism. This coexists, strangely comfortable, with the Enlightenment pretense of a universal humanity, and it leaves out, apparently without a sense of loss, a full appreciation of the communal, the social, the cultural, even the emotional (the inescapable truths of greed and pride, for instance). Consequently, but not surprisingly, enlightened thinking often ends up indulging itself in an orgy of self-doubt, entertaining charges of Laschian if not Kohutian "narcissism" and warnings of the impending collapse of civilized society, if, indeed, this has not already happened, as Alasdair MacIntyre has recently written.

In tribute to Orwell, and in part in criticism of him, I too would like to descend the phylogenetic ladder, not to look at the emerging dictatorship of the mammalian proletariat but rather to look at a more amusing subject—us.

I admit that my anthropomorphic allegory has little of the charm or the subtlety of *Animal Farm*, and certainly none of the genius or originality. It is, however, in the spirit of Orwell, and it has an equally unsettling if not so gloomy ending. Of course, I too would like to set my tale among the domestic pettables—furry or at least fuzzy characters make any story more palatable from the beginning—but Orwell has exhausted the political role of pigs, horses, and donkeys, even if he meanspiritedly denigrates dogs and cats, who in any case already occupy an enviable position in the attention of the popular reading public. A few rungs farther down the ladder, pettability diminishes but sociability and efficiency increase. What might surprise you, however, is that the amount of philosophizing remains more or less constant throughout the animal kingdom. (Plants, on the other hand, prefer deconstructionist criticism.) With this confluence of biology and philosophy, I bring you, as a tribute to Orwell, *Ant Farm*, an allegory about liberalism, the Enlightenment, freedom and individualism, keeping in mind Orwell's belief that only individual values can protect us against totalitarianism. (My apologies to E. O. Wilson for taking such entomological liberties.)

Ant Farm: An Orwellian Allegory

> Ants are so much like human beings as to be an embarrassment. They farm fungi, raise aphids as livestock, launch armies into war, use chemical sprays to alarm and confuse enemies, capture slaves. . . . They exchange information ceaselessly. They do everything but watch television.
>
> —Lewis Thomas, *The Lives of a Cell*

I

The revolution at Harvard Farm was ten generations ago. Though no one remembered the details, everyone knew the story. One night, in Professor Wilson's laboratory, an absentminded graduate student had forgotten to fasten the lid on the terrarium. The queen, her escorts, and the better part of the relatively small nest poured out across the shelves, devouring a couple of cockroaches but otherwise meeting little resistance. At the corner of the cabinet the graduate student had come up suddenly on their rear, recaptured a few dozen workers and, in the frustration of defeat, killed a great many others. But the queen and her escorts had already escaped, even if at a considerable cost.

A few weeks later, no one remembered why they had left the terrarium. The names of the murdered workers were forgotten, but it was remembered that there had been a revolution. The ants had won. There had been terrible losses, but now the nest was once again flourishing, in liberty rather than in slavery. Ants might not have much by way of memory, but they have a keen sense of freedom.

Freedom is what life in an anthill is all about. Thousands of ants die for freedom, virtually every day. They all work for and in freedom, and it is the topic of daily conversations, especially among the males, who have nothing else to do. Their role in the nest, in addition to their occasional sexual favors to the queen, is to keep memory of the revolution and its heritage alive. Since ants have minimal memory, the constant reminders of their liberty are essential.

The males of Harvard Farm were the curators of freedom. "There is no freedom without vigilance," they insisted, though they were never quite sure what it was they were to look out for. They all knew that "freedom is fragile and easily lost," the unspoken presumption, of course, being that they all were free. But, nevertheless, they feared for their freedom, and a few unhappy pessimists argued that they had lost it already.

What you have to understand—what you would certainly think that everyone already understands—is that every ant is different from every other ant. Every ant is unique, with her own personality, her own smell, her own abilities, her own needs. The freedom of the hill was precisely the freedom to develop personality, to smell as one likes (that is, as one is), to realize abilities, to satisfy needs, to help oneself, and, at the same time, to serve queen and colony. The most important thing in life for an ant is self-esteem—which means status in the hill. What ants despise most is dreary uniformity and the banal altruism of most other species. Contrary to certain opinions outside of the hill, every ant works, first of all, for herself, and in competition with every other ant. Indeed, how could it be otherwise? And the collective effort of this competitive selfishness—if you want to call it that—is the energy and efficiency you see in every channel of the nest. (It has been suggested that there is "an invisible antenna" in the colony, a wisdom of organization in the whole that is not necessarily found in any individual ant. But ants, at least, are smart enough to know that this is a suggestive metaphor, nothing more.)

II

Every nest is different from every other nest, and not just in the trivial sense that they are in different places, made of and in different materials and so on. Witness the inevitable warfare that even the most casual contact initiates. And the reason is not hard to discern—smell. A simple, basic difference in smells. Every ant colony has a different smell, a difference in pheromones secreted by the queen. As an ant approaches the nest, that smell means the difference between life and death. Every ant knows every other ant in the colony, not by name of course (only males have names) but by smell. It has been suggested by certain liberals, inside and outside the hill, that the uniqueness of antsmells is merely trivial, that all ants are, "deep down," fundamentally the same. That is a piece of nonsense and is considered by all ants to be both insulting and dangerous. Anyone who smells can smell that every ant is unique, even if some smells are clearly distinctive (not to say superior) to others. Of course one can and sometimes must think in terms of anthood in general, but the beginning and the end of anthood is the unique individual ant. Indeed, the very notion of "anthood" has recently been called into question, for instance, by that ant'ropologist Claude-Levi and by the ant philosopher Jean-Paul. There are no "ants," writes Claude-Levi, there are only drivers, reds, carpenters, "bulldogs," leaf cutters, spider eaters, aphid herders, fungi farmers, and the Disney version. "Ants make themselves," writes Jean-Paul; "whatever is true of us as biological organisms en-soi, every ant has her (or his) autonomy as an ant-pour-soi, the dreadful duty of taking responsibility for our instincts and making them our own (*eigentlichkeit*)."

You will notice that these two great thinkers are males, in a colony that is otherwise entirely made up of females. It is true that all productive roles in the colony are female roles. Yet there are, occasionally, and for brief periods of time, males in the hill. They are the oldest and therefore the wisest members of the hill, having arrived with the queen before any of the workers or soldiers were born (obviously, since one or another of those males was also the father of every ant in the hill). The winged males usually die before the anthill is even founded, but when they live, and they are not needed for food, the colony gladly makes room for them.

Inevitably, an easy life surrounded by hard-working females produces no small number of oddballs among the males. For example, there is Jean-Jacques, who had fought with and alienated every male ant in the hill, and though he frequently mingled with the female workers (often having to run from the soldiers at the same time) he found those relationships equally frustrating and on a number of occasions he had injured female workers in his biologically if not ideologically confused amorousness. Jean-Jacques was forgiven—from a distance—only because of his inspiring vision of natural anthood. In fact, when he was away from the hill—walking through the woods usually—he was in absentia the most popular ant in the hive, favored especially, surprisingly, by the queen.

Then there is Orwell, who also spent most of his time with the females, not wooing but working, in fact, doing the hardest work in the hill, digging new channels and hauling cockroach carcasses from one end of the nest to the other. Consequently, he often found himself on the brink of exhaustion and starvation and extremely bitter toward ants generally, whom he often compared, unfavorably, to aphids and other domestic insects. And yet, Orwell too was generally admired, even liked, by the other ants. He could often be heard to say that he felt inferior to every worker, and he despised the other males, among whom he found "not a single rebel, only cowards, spies and betrayers." Accordingly, Orwell's visions for the future of the colony were dreadful, but they were taken very seriously by a large majority of ants. Indeed, if ants had a calendar, they would readily set a date for the Orwellian apocalypse.

Anthistorians have suggested that the very soul of the colony is to be found not in the queen or the workers but in such odd characters as Jean-Jacques and Orwell. Curiously, we thus find that the celebrities (not heroes or heroines) of antculture often turn out to be those ants who are least part of the colony, least intimate with the activities and loyalties that define the colony, farthest in their thinking from the thoughts and ideals that actually define ant nature (however they try to redefine nature to suit themselves). And, most curiously, they are males, in a culture that is defined by females. But the only ants who can or bother to write anthistory are males, not soldiers or workers. Indeed they are usually odd fellows at that, whose similarities and sympathies with Jean-Jacques and Orwell are obvious. And, of course, the articulate oddball is a convenient vehicle for the symbolism (if not the expression) of individualism, which every ant holds dear. But can you imagine a colony filled with ants such as Jean-Jacques and Orwell?

We might also mention, just in passing, two other such celebrities. There is Franz, a particularly pathetic case, who awakens every morning thinking that he has overnight turned into a human being. Then there is Henry David, who disappeared one day to go into Boston, insisting that a prudent ant in the city did not need a colony to support him. But they are the stuff of literature, hardly of note in the hardworking antworld.

I do not want to give the impression that males are useless. Most males, because they have nothing whatever to do, tend to become the brains of the hill, so to speak. (In fact their brains are no larger than anyone else's.) They provide symbols, amusements, plans for the ultimate revision of the colony. Their job is to design the future, no easy task among animals without a sense of time. They see the "big picture"—not only the colony as a whole (which no other ant, including the queen, has a moment to do), but the entire world of ants and nonants, the world defined and controlled by ants—the antworld. (The history and variety of religions among ants is a fascinating topic that we cannot go into here.) But because of their leisure and their larger view, the males have the awesome duty of defining and protecting freedom, since most of the ants, having little time and no memories, would simply forget that they are free, were not the male ants there to remind them. (When there are no males, it is usually necessary to invent them.)

III

The competitive individualism of ants and their constant concern with status often caused problems within the colony, however "classless" ant society might seem to those who have no place in it. The fact that ants have no concept of "class" and no criteria for status only makes the competition more anxious. Ants were running into and all over one another. Self-proclaimed "realists" (that is, cynics) insisted that antlife is a "jungle," not unlike the truly bug-eat-bug world of some spiders. The competition often divided the hill into de facto groups, usually based on nothing more substantial than some minor matter of smell. Josephine, the queen, routinely worried about questions of class and conflict in the hill. (It is worth remembering that almost all of the ants were immediately related, but competition was no less ferocious for that.) She tried, with some absurdity, to present herself as "one of the girls," her enormous size and singular importance to the hill notwithstanding. In news conferences she always insisted on the equality of all ants. (Ants don't need television, as they are telepathic.) With her public Josephine went out of her way to use popular smells and touches. But this emphasis on equality, unfortunately, only seemed to highlight differences in status, even when it did not diminish the efficiency of the hill.

Among the surviving males, status was a special problem. However ludicrous the queen's egalitarianism, the males had to contend with an even greater absurdity: from the definitive point of view of efficiency and productivity, they were utterly useless and totally expendable. They were well fed and much honored, if also ignored, and virtually nothing was expected from them in return. Accordingly, they found it necessary to continually proclaim the utility of their activities. Consequently, the male ants themselves developed a highly refined and rigid code of "standards" for their behavior, which they used (instead of the more obvious facts of their sex and nonproductivity) to distinguish themselves from all other ants in the hill. (There was considerable uneasiness about the status of the queen in this scheme of things.) This led to a certain tension in the males' ideas and their attitudes toward the colony—a keen sense of their own integrity and superiority to the run-of-the-hill ants mixed with a humiliating sense of their lack of utility and removal from the mainstream of ant activities. Orwell's contempt and

Jean-Jacques's resentment were symptomatic. They couldn't deny the importance of the workers without rejecting the life of the colony, but they couldn't praise the workers without at the same time being painfully aware of their own shortcomings. So even while praising the hardworking females in the hill, they were disdainfully aware of their deficiencies, according to the strict if abstract standards canonized by the males.

This confusion of attitudes always surfaced in the vicious politics among the males, which, though concerned with great questions, had no effect or influence whatever on the rest of the colony. The much-disputed leader of the males—and probable father of the colony—was Napoleon, an unusually small but virile ant whose vitality was something of a legend among the workers and the soldiers. Napoleon, like Josephine, talked about equality all of the time, but unlike the queen, he wore an imperial air. He spoke of the duties of every ant to the hill, and of the better-off ants to help the worse-off ants. "Noblesse oblige," he called it, thus infuriating the more consistently egalitarian ants, particularly Jean-Jacques and Orwell.

Jean-Jacques resented Napoleon's imperial posturing because it seemed to him to be a corruption of natural anthood, made possible by the artificiality of anthill society. It was the individual virtues of the ants that counted, not the false manners of the male ants, whose lives centered on pleasing a too-busy queen and—what was utterly impossible but nevertheless their constant effort—impressing each other. Orwell, on the other hand, despised what he called "the class racket," and though his admiration was directed at the worker ants his contempt was aimed at the informal class divisions among the males themselves, so well symbolized by Napoleon (whose ancestry was reputed to be an ancient and particularly powerful ant farm in Hyannis Port). "All ants may be equal," Orwell would sarcastically comment to whoever would listen, "but some ants are more equal than others." This was generally received as wisdom most profound, summarizing in a phrase both the ideal and the paradox of colony-wide equality. Equality is in evidence, it seems, only to the extent of its absence.

IV

It is often thought that ant colonies are the very paradigm of busy, unreflective, unphilosophical activity. Grasshoppers, for example, who are known for their philosophical opinions but not their prudence or hard work, have long promulgated this misunderstanding. This is, of course, not at all the case. The ant way of life is deeply ideological, whether or not most of the ants have ever thought through their ideology and whether or not they have the

time or the interest to talk about it. It is an ideology of service, but service in
the name of enlightened self-interest, predicated on the indisputable proposition that all ants are both equal and different. They are different in their
abilities. Their tastes and needs are different. Their need to be equal is
unequal. This indisputable proposition, however, provoked a perennial
dispute about power in the colony. Some ants insisted that there was no
power in the colony, apart from the powers of each individual ant. Other ants
argued that the power in the hill was concentrated in the pincers of a few ants
surrounding the queen, though no one knew exactly who they were. More
knowledgeable ants thought that both of these opinions were naïve but had
no better suggestions themselves.

At the founding of the colony, Queen Josephine had insisted confi-
dently that she knew what "her girls really wanted." Whether or not that was
so, the resentment of her maternalism was so great, and not only among the
males, that she ceased saying that altogether and, instead, expressed her
confidence in the individual judgment and choice of each individual ant.
Many ants still suspected Josephine of somehow determining the tastes and
needs of the colony, but as every ant seemed to be making her own decisions,
this suspicion could not even be articulated, much less confirmed. Every ant
had her job, did her job, enjoyed her job, and if it was not true that ants chose
their tasks this was, of course, dictated by the necessities of the hill. Free
choice was the right of every ant in the realm of religion, art, and private life,
and it was one of the pillars of the hill that every ant had the right to speak
as she chose, without fear of punishment. But since ant life was defined by
one's tasks in the hill, these rights—though all-important—did not make
much practical difference. When an ant is defined wholly in terms of her
skills and contributions to the efficiency of the colony, the question of rights,
and of power, would rarely arise, except in the conversations of the males.

Part of the problem, of course, was the dual optics of antlife. The individual was everything, but the life of every ant was defined and made possible
by the colony. An ant alone, it was sometimes said, is not anything at all, a
pitiable creature without a place, without an identity, without a meaning for
her miserable existence. On the other hand, it was obvious that the colony
itself, and anthood in general, were abstractions and nothing whatever
without the multitude of individual ants that populated them. What made
this all the more confusing was the logical fact that the colony possessed
features not attributable to any individual ant or group of ants. Consider, for
example, the much-discussed "roachleg problem": the simple transporting of
a roachleg across the hill: no ant would carry it more than an inch or two,
and no ant had any idea—usually—where the leg was coming from or where
it was going. (The communal fabrication of rumors about such matters was

one of the most enjoyable aspects of antwork.) And yet, the transported load clearly had a destination that was never in question, whether or not it was known by any individual ant. Thus it had sometimes been suggested that the truth is the whole, the activities of the colony and not the individual activities of the ants. But this was almost always dismissed as "totalitarianism." Nothing could be more of a threat to freedom than planning from the top, even the wisest, most benign and uncorrupted planning. Even if individualism failed to explain the rationality of life in the hill, it was preferable to the horrors of totalitarianism. (Ants are very wary of slippery slopes.)

The other side of this argument, however, was best expressed in the morbid view, falsely attributed to Jean-Jacques and Orwell, that ants are irrational and ant life essentially meaningless. This theory preserved the integrity of individualism, but at a terrible—if still acceptable—cost. Except when they are very busy, which luckily is virtually every minute of the day, ants are prone to depression and despair, a matter which some of the males attributed to the degrading nature of most antwork. Whether or not it was planned (and this was a subject of considerable debate) the work of the hill was such that every ant had her inescapable role and place. No one was quite clear whether this was an infringement on freedom, but virtually all of the workers simply accepted it as necessity, indeed, defined what they called "the invertebrate condition" in terms of it. (A popular tale told of a celebrity named Sisyphant, a worker who had spent every day of her life pushing a pebble up a mole hill, only to have it always roll back down again.)

The seemingly inescapable system of things to do was also explained by naturally suspicious ants by reference to an unnamed coterie of powerful ants surrounding the queen. Those who had more faith in anthood proclaimed the system of necessities to be nothing other than the expression of all the collective antwills, guided, as we mentioned before, by "invisible antennae" for the good of all ants. But there was another hypothesis, which dated (as far as anyone knew) back to the earlier incarnation of the colony in Professor Wilson's laboratory. This outrageous hypothesis suggested that the behavior of each individual ant—and consequently the behavior of the colony as a whole—was determined (or at least 78 percent determined) by instincts and "hard-wired" connections in the ants' brains, which in turn were wholly determined by genetics. This would explain the integration of behavior, of course, but the view, popularized as "socioentomology," had one fatal flaw: it left no room—or at any rate too little room (22 percent)—for free will. It was a fact that ants made their own choices. It was a fact that ant society was the result of generations of experimentation and antwisdom. And so the socioentomological hypothesis was treated with utter contempt by virtually every ant. If it could be applied at all, it was suggested by a few sympathetic ants, the socioentomological hypothesis might be appropriate to some of the larger social vertebrates, particularly to those whose large brains and mechanized lives suggested an extraordinary dependence on calculating ability and other complex computerlike functions.

V

As an allegory, the story of Ant Farm lacks several critical ingredients. There is no history, apart from the naked fact of an ancient revolution. And there are no heroes, since, in an important philosophical sense, nothing ever happens. Of course, the ants go on with their work, the queen continues to lay eggs by the hundreds, the males go on arguing. Almost daily, of course, the hill is invaded by wasps and damaged by dogs. Thousands of workers are born and die; new sources of food are discovered and trails are secreted where no ant had ever stepped before. A recent war with the red ants claimed some twelve thousand soldiers, but it was a romantic human observer, no ant, who rhapsodically proclaimed, "For numbers and carnage it was an Austerlitz or a Dresden. Concord fight! . . . I have no doubt that it was a principle they fought for, as much as our ancestors, and not to avoid a three-penny tax on their tea." That human fellow was right, as a matter of fact, about the battle being for principle (more on that in a moment). But he was wrong about its historical importance, for ants have no history. And when the same casual observer declared that "the results of this battle will be as important and memorable to those whom it concerns as those of Bunker Hill, at least," he was clearly anthro- (not ant'ro-) pomorphizing. Ants don't have histories, and so they don't have heroics or heroism.

Ants may not have heroes, but they do have, as we have seen, celebrities—Jean-Jacques and Orwell, for instance, though no one really takes them seriously. This is extremely important to ant life, for where heroes might have some claim to superiority, celebrities do not. Indeed, celebrities are notoriously at the mercy of the most whimsical whims of the most ordinary ants, constant reminders that no ant is really superior to any other ant. (The queen, it is important to note, is never counted as a celebrity.) Most of the current celebrities are male, most of them admired for the sheer sensuality of their bloated abdomens. Only a few, like Jean-Jacques and Orwell, are famed for their ideas, though most ants talk on about their odd personalities. It is one of the peculiarities of antlife that fame and fortune are most often granted to those who contribute *least* to the needs of society. Otherwise, after all, they would not be so readily replaceable.

The emphasis on celebrity should show, once and for all, that ants are not mere utilitarians, concerned with food supplies, colony security, productivity and surplus value and the expansion of their domain. This would be an empty life indeed, and no ant could possibly be satisfied with it. Accordingly, the celebrity system is a vital concern, for it enriches the life of every ant—vicariously, of course—while at the same time keeping everything exactly the same. (Their lack of historical sense notwithstanding, ants tend to be extremely conservative by nature.) One might argue with some persuasiveness that ants live to work and prosper—and to be entertained. (It has even been suggested—most inappropriately—that the queen is too dull for her central place in the hill; accordingly she surrounds herself with antclowns whose sole function is to keep the politics of the colony entertaining.)

VI

It would seem that there are only the brute exigencies of the present moment, and distractions from them. This conclusion, however, is not quite right. In fact, it is entirely mistaken. It is true that ants don't have a sense of historical time; but therefore their sense of the eternal—the timeless—is all the more keen. Ants don't fight for history or tradition (at least, not knowingly) but they do fight for eternal principles. Indeed, if you were to ask any ant—from the soldier whose sole job it is to use her head to plug up an opening to Napoleon, who supposedly coordinates the battle plan of the colony from his cell deep in the hill—she (or he) could not imagine anything else worth fighting for. "For queen and colony." (It has been suggested that the principle of patriotism should be stated, "My colony, right or wrong," but the very idea that one's colony might be wrong is—we should say—deeply unintelligible.)

Antethics is not an ethics of utility, nor even of selfishness, the self-interestedness of ants notwithstanding. Antethics is an ethics of principle. However cynical ants may be about politics, however foolish they may seem in their choice of entertainments and celebrities, one must never underestimate the ultimate importance of antmorality. Ants may not have history, but they do have their eternal principles. "For queen and colony," for example (since there is no conceivable time before, or after, the life of the queen). Some ant principles are extremely general, such as "all ants are equal," and considerable effort is required by the males to state the seemingly endless qualifications, presuppositions and exceptions that such a principle requires. Others are adjustable to the times, such as "Six legs good, eight legs evil," which once was the reigning principle in the days of the spider wars. (We might note that a more recent battle with the centipedes caused considerable confusion, as not even the numbers-minded defense minister, Caspar, had been able to make up a number sufficiently high.)

The essential role of principles in antlife is sometimes misunderstood because, in the hard work of daily life, little time can be spent examining or explaining principles as such, which are usually reduced to simple slogans that every ant is expected to master. Even the brightest ant soon gets perplexed trying to unravel the meaning of "All ants are equal," for example, but not even the dumbest would ever make the mistake of saying that some ants are better than others. So too every ant could be expected to insist that no ant kills another ant without reason, even though in practice this was rather a limited prohibition since the smell of an ant was always a good enough reason to kill her.

Termites and other utilitarian insects do not understand this profound sense of morality shared by all ants. They suggest that such principles are contrary to the ethic of efficiency, but they do not understand that there are values which, to an ant, are more important than mere efficiency. They point out that obedience to moral principles may be contrary to the self-interest that motivates every ant, but any ant can tell you that the interests of the colony and the interests of every ant are one and the same (though no one has ever succeeded in actually proving this). In fact, since every ant desires the well-being of the colony above all else, self-interest and ethics do indeed turn out to be the same. But let us quickly emphasize that this does not mean that ants are ethical "by instinct" or without proper choice in the matter. Ants are free and autonomous creatures who choose as they will as well as choose as they ought to. To insist that ants are "naturally" ethical would be to rob ants of their all-important sense of self-respect and pride.

It seems as if principles have always been the heart of anthood. Indeed, being an ant was even *defined* as acting on principle—working because one believed in the hill, eating because one knew that it was good to eat, cooperating with the other ants in the colony and following the rules because one always knew, according to the great philosopher ant Immanuel, that one should always "act in such a way that the maxim of one's act could be generalized as a universal law for all ants, indeed, for all rational creatures" (presumably that last phrase was meant to include the "lower" insects, if indeed any were rational). If it was pointed out to Immanuel that most ants never thought of such principles, he had simply pointed out that *implicitly* they did so. When it was argued that most ants simply followed a natural, instinctual pattern of behavior, Immanuel angrily retorted that rational anthood and natural inclination were quite distinct, and though instinct might be quite adequate—even necessary—to explain the behavior of less complicated creatures, one had as a matter of rational necessity to assume that every ant was free to reason and rationalize her behavior according to principles. No one in the hill understood exactly what this was supposed to mean, although the queen had evidently considered it very carefully. But the influence of Immanuel in the hill was so great that even those ants who never heard his name believed in the slogan that he had defended: "A good ant is an ant that acts on principle."

VII

The Immanuelian emphasis on principles was intimately tied to the overall emphasis on freedom in the colony and elegantly resolved the paradox of necessity and individual freedom that had plagued some of the more thoughtful ants. It was generally understood and accepted that the safety and wellbeing of the hill required that every ant adhere rather closely to her (and his) established duties, and that minor transgressions of the natural order of the hill must be punished severely, usually with death and dismemberment. But these restrictions were no limitation at all on individual freedom, which, after all, was not a matter of license and permissiveness but rather of free will, that is, the ability to decide to do one's duties in the colony as a rational creature. Very few of the ants understood this—or had thought about it at all—but they all agreed that they did indeed carry out their duties as an act of their own free will and, therefore, were free. Of course, this was only rarely a topic of actual conversation, and then usually among the males. Most of the time, the ants simply enjoyed their freedom, and on collective impulse paraded in long lines along the length of an old log in joyful celebration.

It was this happy harmony of efficiency and freedom, ironically, that formed the foundation of the current crisis in the colony. Ants have two overwhelming fears. They live in fear that they will lose their comfortable lifestyle, and they work themselves to death to make sure that this does not happen. And they fear that they will lose their freedom. No ant can imagine anything worse than an unfree life—a life in which no one had a choice about what to do, a life in which one could not go where one wanted, wear what one wanted to wear (if, that is, one wanted to wear anything), say what one wanted to say. As there was no authority in the hill who threatened such unfreedom, one might think that the ants would be quite content and assured. But the very opposite was the case. Deprived of evident threats to their freedom, they felt compelled to invent them. Indeed, the most radical of the male ants even went so far as to suggest that the affluence and efficiency of the colony—on which ant freedom was based—was itself the source of an insidious unfreedom, an argument which by its very logic turned the ants against themselves. The mood in the hill turned to gloom. Accordingly, Orwell became enormously popular, and Jean-Jacques came to be viewed as an unrealistic optimist by comparison.

Self-deprecation became the ideology of the day. An ant sociologist accused the hill of becoming a "colony of aphids" and a popular writer chastized a whole generation of workers as the "me-decade." The queen herself made a comment about the colony-wide "malaise," and "sickness" became the ruling metaphor for self-perception. An ant historian rumbled the conscience of the hill again with an accusation of "ant narcissism," which just happened to coincide with an unprecedented population boom in which, for the first time, there were more ants than necessary jobs. Thousands of ants saw themselves and their colony as "narcissistic"—though only an ant or two knew what this meant or what was wrong with it. Most recently, a rebellious ant named Alasdair set most of his fellow ants in a tizzy when he declared that civilization had already broken down long ago—indeed, long before the queen and her escorts had even arrived at Harvard Farm. He reminded the ants of their unresolvable disputes; he pointed to the simple-minded phrase making that constituted the supposedly "principled" life of the workers; he lambasted the isolated self-importance of the male ants, who supposed that they directed life in the colony when in fact they supplied at most an otherwise unheard commentary which they argued amongst themselves. Alasdair spoke rhapsodically of the good old days, when every ant knew her place and her virtues, when it was not pretended that every ant had her own unique personality and needs and tastes, when a single spirit of unity held the colony together through even the worst of times. The shame of dubious motives became replaced by the embarrassment of inner emptiness—and the sense of impending doom.

Such talk saddened many ants, while infuriating a few. But no one remembered those good old days, and so life and work went on as usual. Nevertheless, even the most productive ants felt as if they were missing something, as if the truth of life—and freedom—had sneaked by them.

VIII

Harvard Farm still exists, though it has recently moved to the garden behind Kresge Hall of the Business School. The males died, but other males did and would always take up their places and their ideas. Intellectual life too goes on as usual, although the philosophy of the hill now tends to speak more in terms of costs and benefits instead of the older, more idealistic terms of Immanuelian ethics. Cynicism has replaced despair, though it is difficult to tell the difference. *Freedom* is a word that is used more than ever, though its meaning has become increasingly obscure and it has been suggested by the ant songster Kris that it is just another name for "nothing left to lose." Yet even the most cynical ants remain rightly convinced that talking about freedom, no matter how confused, remains the most essential condition for having freedom.

The colony prospers, but it must be said that the ants are not happy. Cyril Connolly caught their plight with an ironic sympathy: "Why do ants alone have parasites whose intoxicating moistures they drink and for whom they will sacrifice even their young? Because as they are the most socialized of insects, so their lives are the most intolerable."

LARAINE FERGENSON

George Orwell's Animal Farm: A Twentieth-Century Beast Fable

*A*nimal Farm, the first of Orwell's books to win him fame and financial security, was also his greatest work of art—a correspondence that does not always occur in the world of literature. Orwell's own comments on *Animal Farm* reveal the high esteem in which he held it. In an often quoted passage of "Why I Write," Orwell asserted, "*Animal Farm* was the first book in which I tried, with full consciousness of what I was doing, to fuse political purpose and artistic purpose into one whole" (*CEJL*, I, 7). He seems to have considered the book his masterpiece, and this is a judgment in which many critics have concurred.

Animal Farm succeeds as a brilliant realization of the beast fable genre. Since this work is longer than the typical fable and since it treats major events over a period of years, it can be termed a beast epic; however, as this discussion will make clear, we can, by considering the work as a fable, explore its elusive underlying meaning, as well as the reasons for its artistic triumph. In this fable Orwell, as he intended, fused the artistic and political purposes of the work, each enhancing the other. It succeeds, moreover, because of the importance of the political purpose itself: its message has apparently struck a responsive chord in its millions of readers.

Yet despite all of these successes, *Animal Farm* has been the subject of many questions—not generally about the artistic merit of the work, but

From *Papers and Fables Read at the Beast Fable Society's Second International Congress Held in Copenhagen, Denmark, 1–7 August 1989.* © 1990 by the Beast Fable Society.

about Orwell's "political purpose" in writing it. Critics have speculated as to the real target of the satire in *Animal Farm*; they have fretted that the work might be misinterpreted; because of its immediate popular success in the cold war period following its publication, they have wondered whether the public was not applauding it for the wrong reasons, that is, seeing it reductively as anti-Communist polemic, a message that Orwell had certainly not intended.

On the surface, the fable seems fairly simple to comprehend. It tells the story of a revolution by farm animals against a cruel master, a revolution eventually corrupted by greed, selfishness, and the lust for power. This revolution and its aftermath are quite pointedly modeled on the Russian Revolution of 1917 and subsequent developments in the Soviet Union up until the mid-forties when Orwell was writing. A long list of correspondences between events in the Soviet Union and events in *Animal Farm* can be made. The Stalin-Trotsky rivalry, leading to the expulsion of Trotsky and Stalin's consolidation of power, is parallelled by the rivalry between the two leading figures of the animals' revolution, Napoleon and Snowball. Snowball, the Trotsky figure, is, like the historical Trotsky, a military leader and a better speaker and theoretician than his rival, Napoleon, who wins through a keener understanding of the nature of power and through sheer ruthlessness. Napoleon has been considered a mixture of Lenin and Stalin. As the one who sequesters puppies and trains them to become a fierce political police force loyal to him, Napoleon may recall Lenin, who formed the Cheka in 1917; but as the satire progresses, Stalin emerges as Orwell's clear target. The rapid industrialization of the Soviet Union under Stalin's prodding is represented by the superhuman—or should we say superanimal—efforts of the farm's residents to build a windmill, which is eventually supposed to increase their standard of living, but which benefits only the pigs. The starvation of the Kulaks who opposed the collectivization of farming has its counterpart in the starvation of the protesting chickens who refused to give up their eggs. The Moscow purge trials are represented by the pitiful confessions and subsequent executions of the animals who opposed Napoleon. The failed pact with Hitler and the disastrous destruction of World War II are reflected in the treachery of neighboring farmer Frederick and the destruction from the Battle of the Windmill. Apart from these detailed correspondences, Orwell's broader satire was, of course, based not specifically on the Russian Revolution, but on any revolution, which could be corrupted by the less desirable aspects of human nature.

Despite the apparent simplicity of this two-level satire—so clear that any bright high school student can grasp it—critics have been profoundly disturbed by what they perceive as the work's actual message, which, we know, need not correspond to the author's intentions. The critics may be correct in their perturbation. There are certain disturbing ambiguities in *Animal Farm*, which can be best explored by examining the work as an example of its genre, the beast fable. By seeing *Animal Farm* in this light and by exploring the role of an apparently minor character, Benjamin the donkey, we can arrive at a profoundly unnerving reading of Orwell's fable.

Orwell wrote *Animal Farm* between November 1943 and February 1944, at a time when the importance of the Anglo-American-Soviet alliance and the military role of the Soviet Union in defeating fascism made any criticism of that nation highly unpopular. Not surprisingly, Orwell had difficulty in finding a publisher for his satire. It was, as he expected, rejected on political grounds by Victor Gollanz, with whom he was still under contract, but with whom he had ideological differences. It was then rejected by the respected firm of Jonathan Cape and after that by Faber and Faber, where T.S. Eliot was editor (Crick, *George Orwell*, 450–458). In a letter to Eliot, Orwell acknowledged that the "meaning" of *Animal Farm* was "not an acceptable one at this moment," but he emphasized that he would make no significant alterations. He mentioned that someone at Cape or the British Ministry of Information had made "the imbecile suggestion that some other animal than pigs might be made to represent the Bolsheviks" (*CEJL* 3:176). Faber too rejected Orwell's masterpiece, but then it was accepted by Secker and Warburg. It made its appearance in August 1945 and promptly sold out (Crick, *George Orwell*, 486). It has been continually reprinted ever since.

Despite the evidence that the book was selling well in England, it was, again on political grounds, rejected by more than a dozen American publishers before Harcourt Brace brought it out. It sold brilliantly in the United States and was even sanctified by the Book-of-the-Month Club (Crick, *George Orwell*, 487–488).

During the frustrating period when Orwell saw his masterpiece rejected again and again, he wrote an essay entitled "The Freedom of the Press," intended to be the preface to *Animal Farm* if and when it was to be published. In this essay, he assailed the cowardice of intellectuals for refusing to enunciate or listen to unpopular opinions. Orwell did not publish this essay with *Animal Farm*, and wisely so, as Bernard Crick has pointed out, for had he included the preface, Crick speculates, "the fable might then have lost its general resonance, might have appeared precisely to be just about Stalin, and the universality of its reflections on the corruption that can come from power might have seemed just the projection of an English literary quarrel" ("How the Essay Came to be Written" 13).

And yet it is the "general resonance" of *Animal Farm* that presents the greatest difficulty. In a 1946 review Louis Ridenour said,

My own pleasure in this satire is greatly reduced by my realization that its object is, as usual, far less the Communist System
than the nature of man himself as this nature has been revealed
in the latter-day development of the Communist system. It is
easy to admire the superb craftmanship with which the attack is
carried out, but it is not comfortable to contemplate the probable
results, in terms of future history, of the traits of human character
elaborated in the satire.

    The message of "*Animal Farm*" seems to be, not that Russia's
leaders have enslaved and exploited their people, though perhaps
they have, but that people are no damn good. (11)

In a similar vein, George Soule, writing in the *New Republic*, complained that
Orwell's intentions were not clear:

Does he mean to say that not these pigs, but Snowball, should
have been on top? Or that the animals should have been merged
in a common primitive communism without leaders or organiza-
tions? . . . or that, as in the old saw criticizing socialism, the possibility of a better society is a pipe-dream, because if property were
distributed equally, the more clever and selfish would soon get a
larger share and things would go on as of old? Though I am sure
he did not intend this moral, the chances are that a sample poll
of the book-club readers in the United States would indicate that
a large majority think so and will heartily approve the book on
that account. (267)

    Soule's questions are quite understandable. Orwell had fought in the
Spanish Civil War with the POUM militia, which had some Trotskyite
connections, and he shared the general opinion that had Trotsky expelled
Stalin instead of the other way around, the world would have witnessed the
emergence of a kinder, gentler Soviet Union. Certainly Snowball appears to
be less brutal and more concerned with the welfare of the other animals than
his rival, Napoleon. Nonetheless, the text itself and Orwell's comments on it
clearly indicate that he did not intend *Animal Farm* as a Trotskyite tract. The
first sign of the betrayal of the revolution is the pigs' appropriation of the
milk and apples for themselves instead of sharing them among all of the
animals. Orwell says in *Animal Farm*, "All the pigs were in full agreement on
this point, even Snowball and Napoleon" (42). Orwell marked this section of
the book in a copy that he gave to a friend and told him that it was "the key
passage" (Crick, *George Orwell*, 490), and he also cited it in a conversation

with Julian Symons as evidence that "Trotsky-Snowball was potentially as big a villain as Stalin-Napoleon . . ." (Woodcock 196). Thus, whatever Orwell's intended message in *Animal Farm*, it was not a Trotskyite one.

But, having rejected the Trotskyite view, we return to the question: What is *Animal Farm*'s true message? Actually, as long as one keeps carefully to certain generalities or to certain specifics, there seems to be really no problem in answering this question.

Despite *Animal Farm*'s ambiguities, certain general messages seem clear: Power corrupts; Passivity is dangerous; Freedom, dearly won, may be lost; Political movements with just goals that attract idealistic people may turn evil. We might also find fairly clear a few specific points: The Russian Revolution, noble in its inception, was a revolution betrayed by the greed, cruelty, and lust for power of its leaders, specifically Stalin, and also by the inability of the Russian people and communist insiders to oppose him effectively; Socialism, which had held out the promise of a better life for the great majority of people, and had lured many idealists, had degenerated in the particular case of Russian Communism into a means of oppression. These "meanings"—elaborations of those we began with—are all seemingly unarguable, but they did not, and do not, satisfy the interpreters of this work. Why do we seek more?

I would like to suggest two reasons. and these are related to each other. One is that the above interpretations are static. To paraphrase Orwell from *Nineteen Eighty-Four*, they explain to some extent the *how*— but not the *why* (145). They may offer a reading, a *how* to read the work. But *Why*, the critics, kept—and keep—asking, *did this happen, or does it happen*? Is it inevitable that socialist revolutions will be betrayed, as the Soviet one was because of some innate human defect or some innate flaw in socialism? The second reason for the discontent with the messages above relates to the genre of the work—the beast fable.

Here I would like to comment on Jan Ziolkowski's intriguing statement that "*Animal Farm* is not a beast fable, but it resembles a fable in its economy of style and its use of animals to attack a group that could not be attacked openly." The lack of a clear moral is a good argument for this view, and it may well explain Orwell's own apparent rejection of the term "fable" that is implied by his addition of the subtitle—which he did not have to provide at all—with the morally ambiguous term "A Fairy Story." In his preface to the Signet edition, C. M. Woodhouse discusses Orwell's use of this term to fit a story that seems to have no moral; that is, evil is not punished and virtue is not rewarded in *Animal Farm*. According to Woodhouse, Orwell's "message (which is by no means a moral) is that of all the great fairy stories: 'Life is like that—take it or leave it'" (xii).

In an insightful letter to Orwell, the critic William Empson praised the work for its beautiful prose style, but warned that it might be misunderstood. Pointing out that his son found it "very strong Tory propaganda," Empson continued:

> Your point of view of course is that the animals ought to have gone on sharing Animal Farm. But the effect of the farmyard, with its unescapable racial differences, is to suggest that the Russian scene had unescapable social differences too—so the metaphor suggests that the Russian revolution was always a pathetically impossible attempt. To be sure, this is denied by the story because the pigs can turn into men, but the story is far from making one feel that any of the other animals could have turned into men. . . .
>
> I certainly don't mean that that is a fault in the allegory; it is a form that has to be set down and allowed to grow like a separate creature, and I think you let it do that with honesty and restraint. But I thought it worth warning you . . . that you must expect to be 'misunderstood' on a large scale about this book; it is a form that inherently means more than the author means, when it is handled sufficiently well. (Qtd. in Crick, *George Orwell*, 491–492)

Empson's warning, as we have seen, was certainly borne out by subsequent events. And by talking about the "form" of the work having a life of its own and taking on its own meaning, he points out precisely why an analysis of Orwell's work as a beast fable is so useful.

Contradicting Ridenour's view, cited earlier, that *Animal Farm* teaches that people are no good, Orwell portrays many of the animals as noble, unselfish, and self-sacrificing. Unfortunately, these are not the animals with the intelligence to place them in leadership positions. Brains seem to be the monopoly—or as we shall see, the near monopoly—of the least moral animals on the farm—the selfish, power-mad pigs. Orwell says pointedly of Boxer, the noble workhorse representing the common laboring classes, that "he was not of first-rate intelligence" (16)—an estimation that is illustrated when the horse, despite great efforts, can retain no more than four letters of the alphabet (40). Furthermore, the satire becomes painful as Boxer, along with the other animals, accepts the lies of Squealer, the pigs' propaganda minister: their revision of history and their rationalizations for violating all of the principles of the revolution. All of Boxer's doubts are settled by his blind faith in Comrade Napoleon (81) and in his determination to work harder (84).

Even Snowball, who despite his flaws, is preferable to Napoleon and who seems (like this historical Trotsky) to have a more subtle intellect than his rival, is out-foxed—or should we say out-dogged—by him and loses the power struggle owing to Napoleon's superiority in practical strategy and to his greater ruthlessness. Thus, allegorically, Orwell seems to be saying not that people are no good, but that the most vicious and selfish of people often (or is it always?) gain control over their moral betters.

If Orwell's use of the beast fable creates an intriguingly ambiguous, but ultimately pessimistic message, it is also a reason for the work's vividness and power to engage the reader. J. R. Hammond cites the work's "incomparable success as a beast fable" (163) and Orwell's feeling of empathy for animals, which was one of his lifelong characteristics, as sources of its popularity and appeal (163–164). Hammonds also notes Orwell's humor (165), and this is a curious feature of so pessimistic a work. Satirizing the communist and socialist penchant for forming committees, Orwell writes of Snowball, during the early stages when Animal Farm still held out hope, as being an "indefatigable" organizer:

> He formed the Egg Production Committee for the Hens, the Clean Tails League for the cows, the Wild Comrades' Re-education Committee (the object of this was to tame the rats and rabbits), the Whiter Wool Movement for the sheep, and various others. . . . (39)

Even when Orwell describes the unhappy outcome of all of these committees in a way that reinforces the pessimism of the book, he does so with a charm and humor that are hard to resist:

> On the whole, these projects were a failure. The attempt to tame the wild creatures, for instance, broke down almost immediately. They continued to behave very much as before, and when treated with generosity, simply took advantage of it. The cat joined the Re-education Committee and was very active in it for some days. She was seen one day sitting on a roof and talking to some sparrows who were just out of reach. She was telling them that all animals were now comrades and that any sparrow who chose could come and perch on her paw; but the sparrows kept their distance. (39)

Following this passage, Orwell says ironically that the reading and writing classes were "a great success," but it soon becomes clear that this success does not extend to Boxer and the majority of the animals. They remain in ignorance, passive victims to the pigs' machinations and exploitation.

Orwell's use of the beast fable form allowed him to state this depressing view of human relations indirectly, but he has raised the issue of a grim future for humanity directly enough in some of his essays, for example in "Looking Back on the Spanish War," and it is the theme of his last work, often considered his most despairing—the apocalyptic *Nineteen Eighty-Four*.

But in *Nineteen Eighty-Four*, as in "Looking Back on the Spanish War," which is closely related to it, one is aware of a constant tension or dialectic between the famous Orwellian pessimism and a less often noted optimism. Orwell had glimpsed a truly egalitarian society in Spain, and even though he saw that society destroyed, he clung to that inspiring vision. Orwell believed, at least with one part of his mind, that the working class, the proles, were a reliable enemy of fascism, more reliable than the intelligentsia, who could be bribed either ideologically or simply with the promise of superior wealth, or who would wither in defeat when realizing the odds against them. Sometimes the naiveté of the proletariat seemed to Orwell to be its strength: it was he said, like a plant, that blindly and stupidly keeps pushing toward the sun (*CEJL* 2: 260–261). But in *Nineteen Eighty-Four*, we find the pessimistic formulation that the proles cannot overthrow the dictatorship because they lack political consciousness (48, 174).

In *Animal Farm*, the one animal outside the porcine ruling clique that seems to have the intelligence to warn the others of what is happening to them is Benjamin the donkey. He can read as well as any pig, but chooses not to use his ability, until it is too late. Throughout the story, Benjamin plays the role of the uninvolved intellectual, very much the type that Orwell had criticized in his essay "Inside the Whale," in which he characterizes certain writers (chief among them Henry Miller) as committing the sin of Jonah—refusing to preach to the people of Ninevah and being encapsulated in the belly of the whale, a metaphor for the uninvolved artist or intellectual cut off from society. Benjamin the donkey, rejecting the principles of animalism because of a deep-rooted pessimism that—as Orwell often feared it might—manifested itself in political quietism, refuses to believe that life can be made better. Things will go on as they always have, he asserts—and that is badly (55–56). He generally refuses to read when the non-literate animals ask him to—even to help the animals understand vital issues such as the pigs' subversion of the basic Seven Commandments of Animalism (88).

But Benjamin makes one notable exception: he alerts the other animals that the pigs have treacherously sold Boxer to the knackers (horseslaughterer) when the devoted beast is too old and ill to be exploited by them any further. Significantly, Benjamin's intercession is too late to save his friend.

When the pigs "explain" to the other animals that a mistake has been made because the veterinary surgeon who took Boxer away had recently purchased his van from the knacker and had not yet changed its sign, the animals are "enormously relieved." They believe the lies of Squealer, the pig who functions as the ministry of propaganda, and attend a memorial ceremony at which Napoleon regrets that it is not possible to have Boxer's remains brought back for burial at the farm, but reminds the other animals of the horse's two mottos, "I will work harder" and "Comrade Napoleon is always right" (113–116). Orwell ends this section of the book with a paragraph describing a drunken revel in the farmhouse, now occupied by the pigs, and the laconic statement that "from somewhere or other the pigs had acquired the money to buy themselves another case of whisky" (116). Benjamin does not even attempt to enlighten the other animals to the truth, but after the death of Boxer, his only friend, he becomes "more morose and taciturn than ever" (117).

As mentioned earlier, although *Animal Farm* can be considered a "beast epic," the term "fable" more clearly illuminates the interpretive problems it presents. A fable may be defined as "A short tale, usually epigrammatic, with animals, men, or gods . . . as characters. The action of a fable illustrates a moral which is usually (but not always) explicitly stated at the end. This moral often attains the force of a proverb" (Benet 333). We know from the previous analysis that *Animal Farm* certainly does not have one clear moral, but there is, in fact, a proverb near its conclusion. When the animals, totally disillusioned at seeing the pigs on two legs and indistinguishable from the human masters they thought had been overthrown, return to the wall that once contained the Seven Commandments of Animalism, all of which have been subverted, they find instead just one sentence—the chilling "ALL ANIMALS ARE EQUAL BUT SOME ANIMALS ARE MORE EQUAL THAN OTHERS" (123). This motto is what the pigs have written in place of the Seven Commandments, and we, of course, need not take it as Orwell's final statement. It is, nevertheless, this basic inequality that has subverted the revolution, as Empson, in the letter I cited earlier, pointed out.

Orwell, despite a lifetime of writing, working, and fighting for equality, had grave doubts about it as a political force. He never totally overcame the early indoctrination in snobbery that he acquired from his "lower-upper-middle class" background (Orwell, *The Road to Wigan Pier*, 121) and his upper-class education. Thus, the not so hidden message of *Animal Farm* is not that human beings are not capable of great kindness, nobility, and sacrifice, but that basic inequalities may make these virtues insufficient to guarantee freedom.

The beast fable has often been a means of veiling social and political criticism. Certainly Orwell's use of the genre to cloak an attack on Stalin was motivated by the necessity of not directly assailing him as he was playing a crucial role in the world's struggle against Nazism. But the allegory did not hide Orwell's anti-Stalinism: the satire's application to the Soviet Union was so obvious that one might well ask whether Orwell had another motive for choosing this form. Perhaps it was to hide—even from himself—a more subversive message, one that undermined not just the Anglo-Soviet alliance, but the nature of democracy itself.

This unique work seems to imply that the masses cannot save themselves from would-be exploiters: they need the leadership of intellectuals. But intellectuals, unfortunately, can be cowed and defeated, like some of the pigs; bribed and corrupted like most of the pigs; or hopelessly cynical, and hence uninvolved and irresponsible, like Benjamin the donkey. The beast fable medium allows Orwell to put forth this pessimistic message in a veiled and engaging way, but it has troubled commentators since the work's publication and no doubt will continue to do so.

V.C. LETEMENDIA

Revolution on *Animal Farm*:
Orwell's Neglected Commentary

In the last scene of George Orwell's "fairy tale," *Animal Farm*, the humbler animals peer through a window of the farmhouse to observe a horrible sight: the pigs who rule over them have grown indistinguishable from their temporary allies, the human farmers, whom they originally fought to overthrow. The animals' fate seems to mirror rather closely that of the common people as Orwell envisaged it some six years before commencing *Animal Farm*: "what you get over and over again is a movement of the proletariat which is promptly canalized and betrayed by astute people at the top, and then the growth of a new governing class. The one thing that never arrives is equality. The mass of the people never get the chance to bring their innate decency into the control of affairs, so that one is almost driven to the cynical thought that men are only decent when they are powerless." Obviously *Animal Farm* was designed to parody the betrayal of Socialist ideals by the Soviet regime. Yet it has also been interpreted by various readers as expressing Orwell's own disillusion with any form of revolutionary political change and, by others, as unfolding such a meaning even without its author's conscious intention. It is time now to challenge both of these views.

Orwell himself commented of *Animal Farm* that "if it does not speak for itself, it is a failure." The text does indeed stand alone to reveal Orwell's consistent belief not only in democratic Socialism, but in the possibility of a

From *Journal of Modern Literature* 18:1 (Winter 1992). © 1994 by Temple University.

democratic Socialist revolution, but there is also a considerable body of evidence outside *Animal Farm* that can be shown to corroborate this interpretation. The series of events surrounding its publication, and Orwell's own consistent attitude towards his book provide evidence of its political meaning. Meanwhile, of the two extant prefaces written by Orwell, the one designed for the Ukrainian edition, composed in 1947, is of particular political interest. Orwell's correspondence with his friends and acquaintances on the subject of *Animal Farm* provides a further source of information. Some of these letters are well known to Orwell scholars, but his correspondence with Dwight Macdonald, with whom he became friends when he was writing for the American journal, *Partisan Review*, does not appear to have been fully investigated. Macdonald himself raised a direct question about the political intent of *Animal Farm* and was given a specific answer by Orwell, yet this fascinating evidence has apparently been neglected, in spite of the generous access now available to his correspondence in the Orwell Archive.

Commentators on Orwell find it easy to conclude from *Animal Farm* the utter despair and pessimism either of its author, or of the tale itself. It must be remembered, however, that through his allegory Orwell plays a two-sided game with his reader. In some ways, he clearly emphasizes the similarities between the beasts on *Animal Farm* and the humans whom they are designed to represent; at other times, he demonstrates with both humor and pathos the profound differences separating animal from man—differences which in the end serve to limit the former. In doing so, he forces his reader to draw a distinction between the personalities and conduct of the beasts and those of the human world. Of course, the animals are designed to represent working people in their initial social, economic, and political position in the society not just of *Animal Farm* but of England in general. The basic antagonism between working class and capitalist is also strongly emphasized by the metaphor: pig and man quarrel fiercely at the end of the story. The diversity of the animal class, like the working class, is equally stressed by the differing personalities of the creatures. Just because all have been subjected to human rule, this does not mean that they will act as a united body once they take over the farm. The qualities which, for Orwell, clearly unite the majority of the animals with their human counterparts, the common working people, are a concern for freedom and equality in society and a form of "innate decency" which prevents them from desiring power for any personal gain. While this decency hinders the worker animals from discovering the true nature of the pigs until the final scene, it also provides them with an instinctive feeling for what a fair society might actually look like. Yet Orwell was obviously aware, in using this metaphor, that the animals differ fundamentally from their human counterparts. Unlike men, the majority of the beasts are limited naturally by their brief lifespan and the consequent shortness of their memory. Moreover, their differentiated physical types deny them the versatility of humans. Their class structure is fixed by their immutable functions on the farm: a horse can never fill the role of a hen. The class structure of human society, in contrast, is free from such biological demarcations. These two profoundly limiting aspects of the animal condition, in which men share no part, finally contribute to the creatures' passivity in the face of the pig dictatorship. The metaphor, then, cannot be reduced to a simple equivalence, in the way that the pigs reduce the seven Commandments of *Animal Farm* to one.

Evidently the animals lack education and self-confidence in spite of the active role which most of them played in the first rebellion and, in the case of some, are naturally stupid. Orwell is not implying by this the hopelessness of a proletarian revolution: he rather points to the need for education and self-confidence in any working class movement if it is to remain democratic in character. Both of these attributes, he appears further to suggest, must come from within the movement itself. The crude proletarian spirit of the common animals necessarily provides the essential ingredient for a revolution towards a free and equal society, but it needs careful honing and polishing if it is not to fall victim to its own inherent decency and modesty. If this simple, instinctive decency is to be preserved in the transition from revolution—which is all too easy—to the construction of a new society— which is not—other kinds of virtue are also necessary and must at all costs be developed by the working class if it is not to be betrayed again. The text itself, however, hints at disaster for the rule of the pigs. Their single tenet asserting that some animals are more equal than others is in the end a meaningless absurdity. In spite of their great intellectual gifts, the pigs are ultimately the most absurd of all the farm animals, for they are attempting to assume a human identity which cannot belong to them. It is left to the reader to ponder the potential for political change, given the evident weakness and vanity at the core of the pig dictatorship. The final scene of the book, moreover, reveals the disillusionment of the working beasts with their porcine leaders, an essential step in the process of creating a new revolution.

Evidence external to the text of *Animal Farm* is not required to establish the political meaning within its pages. Yet an examination of Orwell's attitude towards the book during the difficult period in which he tried to have it published only strengthens the conclusions drawn here. Even before *Animal Farm* was finished, Orwell was quite aware that it would cause controversy because of its untimely anti-Stalinist message, and he predicted difficulties in publishing it. He was, of course, correct: the manuscript was refused by Gollancz, Andre Deutsch, and Jonathan Cape—in the latter case on the advice of the Ministry of Information. Meanwhile, Orwell declined an offer to publish the book in serial form in Lady Rhondda's *Time and Tide*, explaining that the politics of the journal were too right-wing for his tale, only to be turned down by T.S. Eliot at Faber and Faber, his next choice of publisher. The end of the story is well known to Orwell scholars: Orwell went finally to Frederick Warburg, who accepted the manuscript, and upon its publication in August 1945, it was well received and soon selected by the Book-of-the-Month Club. Orwell's interest in the major publishing houses, as well as his reluctance to approach Frederick Warburg as a first choice and his willingness at one desperate point to pay himself to have the work reproduced in pamphlet form show that he wanted it to reach the public at all costs and to address as wide an audience as possible from as unprejudiced a political context as he could find. Naturally, Lady Rhondda's journal would not have been suitable: his purpose was not to congratulate conservatives or even liberals on the failure of the Russian Revolution, however scathing his criticism of the Stalinist regime within the allegory. Furthermore, Orwell stood firmly against any suggested alterations to the text, particularly in the instance of his representation of the Bolsheviks as pigs. He made no excuses for *Animal Farm*—as he would in the case of *Nineteen Eighty-Four*—and must have considered its message to be fairly clear, for he offered no press releases to correct misinterpretations of the book from either right- or left-wing political camps. On the contrary, it rather seems that he was proud of the quality, as much as the political timeliness, of the book and expected it to require no external defence or explanation; this opinion did not appear to change.

Some further indication of Orwell's own view of *Animal Farm* may be found in the two prefaces he wrote for it. Of the two, only the Ukrainian preface was actually published. Its original English version, written early in 1947, has never been found, and only a translation from the Ukrainian is available to Orwell scholars. This presents the possibility that various errors or subtle alterations of meaning might have remained uncorrected by the author when it was first translated from English to Ukrainian. Written two years after the English preface, the Ukrainian piece obviously betrays a purpose very different from that of its predecessor, as a result supplying the reader with far more direct commentary on the text. Orwell makes it clear here that he "became pro-Socialist more out of disgust with the way the poorer section of the industrial workers were oppressed and neglected than out of any theoretical admiration for a planned society." His experiences in Spain, he states, gave him first-hand evidence of the ease with which "totalitarian propaganda can control the opinion of enlightened people in democratic countries." Not only were the accusations against Trotskyists in Spain the same as those made at the Moscow trials in the USSR; Orwell considers that he "had every reason to believe that [they] were false," as far as Spain was concerned. Upon his return to England, he discovered "the numerous sensible and well-informed observers believing the most fantastic accounts of conspiracy, treachery and sabotage which the press reported from the Moscow trials." What upset him most was not the "barbaric and undemocratic methods" of Stalin and his associates, since, he argues, "It is quite possible that even with the best intentions, they could not have acted otherwise under the conditions prevailing there." The real problem, in his view, was that Western Europeans could not see the truth about the Soviet regime, still considering it a Socialist country when, in fact, it was being transformed "into a hierarchical society, in which the rulers have no more reason to give up their power than any other ruling class." Both workers and the intelligentsia had to be disabused of this illusion which they held partly out of wilful misunderstanding and partly because of an inability to comprehend totalitarianism, "being accustomed to comparative freedom and moderation in public life." To make possible, then, a "revival of the Socialist movement" by exposing the Soviet myth, Orwell writes that he tried to think of "a story that could be easily understood by almost everyone and which could be easily translated into other languages."

He claims that although the idea came to him upon his return from Spain in 1937, the details of the story were not worked out until the day he "saw a little boy, perhaps ten years old, driving a huge cart-horse along a narrow path, whipping it whenever it tried to turn." If the horse could only become aware of its own strength, the boy would obviously have no control over it. Orwell found in this a parallel with the way in which "the rich exploit the proletariat," and he proceeded from this recognition "to analyse Marx's argument from the animals' point of view." For them, he argues, the idea of class struggle between humans was illusory; the real tension was between animals and men, "since whenever it was necessary to exploit animals, all humans united against them." The story was not hard to elaborate from this, Orwell continues, although he did not actually write it all out until 1943, some six years after the main ideas had been conceived of. Orwell declines to comment on the work in his preface, for "if it does not speak for itself, it is a failure." Yet he ends with two points about details in the story: first, that it required some chronological rearrangement of the events of the Russian Revolution, and, second, that he did not mean pigs and men to appear reconciled completely at the end of the book. On the contrary, "I meant it to end on a loud note of discord, for I wrote it immediately after the Teheran Conference [parodied by the final scene in *Animal Farm*] which everybody thought had established the best possible relations between the USSR and the West. I personally did not believe that such good relations would last long. . . ."

It seems, then, that as much as Orwell wanted to explain how he had arrived at Socialism and at his understanding of totalitarianism, he sought to indicate in this preface to Ukrainian readers how workers and intelligentsia in Western Europe, but especially in England, misperceived the difference between the Soviet Union of 1917 and that of twenty and thirty years later. *Animal Farm* was, according to its author, an attempt to strip away the mythical veil shrouding the Stalinist regime; simultaneously, however, he was trying to renew what had been lost through this deception and to revive the original spirit of the Socialist movement. It seems possible to conclude that Orwell is suggesting the presence of just such a double intention within the allegory. One point in the preface, however, requires clarification. Orwell's reference to the animals' view that the real class struggle lay between animals and humans suggests, in the context of the allegory, the absence of any significant class struggle between members of the ruling class—or humans—since they will readily forget their differences and unite to oppress animals. This appears confusing when applied to Marx's theory, which Orwell claims as the theoretical basis of this insight, and furthermore it does not capture the thrust of the story itself, in which the divisions between animals are exposed in detail, rather than those between humans, or even between humans and animals. But Orwell makes it quite clear here that he refers to an animal perspective in defining the class struggle as one between humans and beasts. Certainly the point of departure was, in both the Russian situation and in this particular allegory, the identification and removal of the most evident class of oppressors. In this initial movement, the oppressed class was not mistaken politically; what came afterwards in both instances, though, demonstrated that the first movement of revolutionary consciousness had not been sustained in its purity, since the goals of the revolution gradually began to be violated. Orwell's remark in the preface that "[f]rom this point of departure [the animals' view of the class struggle], it was not difficult to elaborate the rest of the story" cannot be taken as an admission that the animals' perspective was perfectly correct. Of course, the book debunks such a simplistic interpretation of the class struggle, in spite of its initial accuracy.

By revealing the divisions within the animal ranks, Orwell is cautioning his reader to question the animal view of the class struggle, for the crucial problem that even the wise Old Major does not predict in his identification of the real enemy is the power-hunger of the pigs. By allegorical implication, this points rather interestingly to Orwell's identification of a flaw in the Marxian theory of revolution itself. Although its starting point is clearly the animals' partially accurate but insufficient analysis of the class struggle, the allegory in its course reveals more and more drastically the inadequacy of such a view as a basis for post-revolutionary society. Part of Old Major's vision is indeed debunked, while the truth of the initial insight about class struggle is never denied, and the story, as has been seen, ends on a note of hope. Orwell's final point in the preface constitutes the only correction and very mild apology that he would make about the text, even though he had had roughly two years to assess the critical response—and hence the variety of misinterpretations—circulating about *Animal Farm*. Here he is warning his reader about the subtlety of his allegory: pigs and humans may come to look the same at the end, but they are still essentially enemies and share only a greed for power. For it is indeed the dispute between farmers and pigs which completes the transformation of pig to man and of man to pig.

If the Ukrainian preface was written for an unknown audience, the English preface was designed for readers with whom Orwell was much more familiar. Written in 1945, when he was still bitterly upset over the difficulties of printing unpopular political commentary in wartime Britain, the English preface is concerned not with the content of the story but with the question of whether he would be free to publish it at all because of current political alliances, intellectual prejudices, and general apathy over the need to defend basic democratic liberties. Attacking as he does here the political toadying of the Left intelligentsia in Britain to the Stalinist regime, Orwell presents *Animal Farm* as a lesson for the well-educated as much as the uneducated. Meanwhile, the fact that he makes no reference in this preface to the details of the book indicates his strong confidence in its political clarity for English readers, although his bitter tone shows, as Crick suggests, Orwell's acute sense that he was being "persecuted for plain speaking" before *Animal Farm* was published. Since the English preface does not actually offer an interpretation of *Animal Farm* explaining Orwell's political intention, it is necessary to look for this information in his more private communications on the subject.

Orwell commented explicitly on his book to his friends Geoffrey Gorer and Dwight Macdonald. Crick states that Orwell gave a copy of *Animal Farm* to Gorer having marked in it the passage in which Squealer defends the pigs' theft of the milk and apples. He told Gorer that this "was the key passage." This emphasis of Orwell's is reiterated and explained more fully in a letter to Dwight Macdonald written shortly after *Animal Farm* first appeared in the United States, in 1946. Macdonald was one of a group of American intellectuals who had broken with Soviet Communism as early as 1936 and had gone to work with Philip Rahv and William Phillips on *Partisan Review*. From January 1941 to the summer of 1946, Orwell had sent regular "letters" to the review and had had cause to correspond with Macdonald fairly frequently.

Macdonald was later to move to the editorship of *Politics*, described by
Orwell in a letter to T.S. Eliot as "a sort of dissident offshoot" of *Partisan
Review*, and had already championed a review written by Orwell that had
been rejected for political reasons by the *Manchester Evening News*. This
shared political understanding soon developed into a literary friendship
which lasted until Orwell's death in 1950.

In September 1944, Orwell had already written to Macdonald
expressing his views about the Soviet Union. Given that only a few months
separated the completion of *Animal Farm* from this letter, it seems safe to
assume that the views expressed in both might be similar. To Macdonald,
Orwell stated, "I think the USSR is the dynamo of world Socialism, so long
as people believe in it. I think that if the USSR were to be conquered by
some foreign country the working class everywhere would lose heart, for the
time being at least, and the ordinary stupid capitalists who never lost their
suspicion of Russia would be encouraged." Furthermore, "the fact that the
Germans have failed to conquer Russia has given prestige to the idea of
Socialism. For that reason I wouldn't want to see the USSR destroyed and
think it ought to be defended if necessary." There is a caution, however:
"[b]ut I want people to become disillusioned about it and to realise that they
must build their own Socialist movement without Russian interference, and
I want the existence of democratic Socialism in the West to exert a regenerative influence upon Russia." He concludes that "if the working class everywhere had been taught to be as anti-Russian as the Germans have been made,
the USSR would simply have collapsed in 1941 or 1942, and God knows
what things would then have come out from under their stones. After that
Spanish business I hate the Stalin regime perhaps worse than you do, but I
think one must defend it against people like Franco, Laval etc."

In spite of its repressive features and its betrayal of basic human free-
doms, then, Orwell still considered the Soviet regime to be vital as an
example to the working class everywhere. The real danger lay in the idea that
it defined Socialism. What was most needed was a new form of democratic
Socialism created and maintained by the people. He offers meanwhile the
possibility that such democratic forms of Socialism elsewhere might actually
have a benign effect on the Russian regime. In the allegorical context of
Animal Farm, Napoleon's dictatorship would still seem to be a step forward
from that of the human farmers—according to Orwell's letter, the rule of
"the ordinary stupid capitalists." For animals outside the farm, it would
provide a beacon of hope—so long as the truth about the betrayal taking
place within was made plain to them. For it would now become their task to
build their own movement in a democratic spirit which might, in Orwell's
words, "exert a regenerative influence" on the corruption of the pigs' realm.

When *Animal Farm* finally appeared in the United States in 1946, Macdonald wrote again to Orwell, this time to discuss the book: "most of the anti-Stalinist intellectuals I know . . . don't seem to share my enthusiasm for *Animal Farm*. They claim that your parable means that revolution always ends badly for the underdog, hence to hell with it and hail the status quo. My own reading of the book is that it is meant to apply to Russia without making any larger statement about the philosophy of revolution. None of the objectors have so far satisfied me when I raised this point; they admit explicitly that is all you profess to do, but still insist that implicit is the broader point. . . . Which view would you say comes closer to your intentions?"

Orwell's reply deserves quoting in full: "Of course I intended it primarily as a satire on the Russian revolution. But I did mean it to have a wider application in so much that I meant that that kind of revolution (violent conspiratorial revolution, led by unconsciously power-hungry people) can only lead to a change of masters. I meant the moral to be that revolutions only effect a radical improvement when the masses are alert and know how to chuck out their leaders as soon as the latter have done their job. The turning point of the story was supposed to be when the pigs kept the milk and apples for themselves (Kronstadt.) If the other animals had had the sense to put their foot down then, it would have been all right. If people think I am defending the status quo, that is, I think, because they have grown pessimistic and assume there is no alternative except dictatorship or laissez-faire capitalism. In the case of the Trotskyists, there is the added complication that they feel responsible for events in the USSR up to about 1926 and have to assume that a sudden degeneration took place about that date, whereas I think the whole process was foreseeable—and was foreseen by a few people, e.g. Bertrand Russell—from the very nature of the Bolshevik party. What I was trying to say was, 'You can't have a revolution unless you make it for yourself; there is no such thing as a benevolent dictatorship.'"

Yes, *Animal Farm* was intended to have a wider application than a satire upon the Russian regime alone. Yes, it did indeed imply that the rule of the pigs was only "a change of masters." Yet it did not condemn to the same fate all revolutions, nor for a moment suggest that Farmer Jones should be reinstated as a more benevolent dictator than Napoleon. According to Orwell's letter, the problem examined by *Animal Farm* concerns the nature of revolution itself. Unless everyone makes the revolution for him or herself without surrendering power to an elite, there will be little hope for freedom or equality. A revolution in which violence and conspiracy become the tools most resorted to, one which is led by a consciously or unconsciously power-hungry group, will inevitably betray its own principles. Failing to protest when the pigs kept the milk and apples for themselves, the other animals surrendered what power they might have had to pig leadership. Had they been "alert and [known] how to chuck out their leaders" once the latter had fulfilled their task, the original spirit of *Animal Farm* might have been salvaged. The book itself, Orwell makes clear in his letter, was calling not for the end of revolutionary hopes, but for the beginning of a new kind of personal responsibility on the part of revolutionaries. The most important barrier in the way of such a democratic Socialist revolution was the Soviet myth: if people outside still thought that that particular form of revolution could succeed without betraying its goals, nothing new could be accomplished. The final note of Orwell's letter is optimistic: if people mistook his message for a conservative one, it was precisely their problem. They had no confidence in the possibility of an alternative to either capitalism or dictatorship. In a sense, they would be like those animals who, when forced into making a choice between a false set of alternatives by Squealer—either the return of Farmer Jones or unquestioning obedience to the rule of the pigs—failed to consider the possibility of a third choice, a democratic Socialist society. For although Orwell was prepared to provide a fairly detailed explanation of his animal story for his friend Macdonald, his letter makes it quite evident that the burden of understanding *Animal Farm* still lay with its reader.

Given the striking congruity between the text and Orwell's political commentary about it, it would be rash to argue that he had lost control of his allegory in *Animal Farm*. If it takes time and effort to expose the political intricacies behind the stark prose of his animal fable, this must have been partly his intention: the lesson of democracy was not an easy one to learn, and the next revolutionary move towards democratic Socialism could surely not be allowed to repeat the mistakes of Old Major. Still, we may wonder if the grain of hope provided by the final scene of the book is not, in this light, too insubstantial to feed a new generation of revolutionaries. Yet if Orwell had presented an easy political resolution to the horrors of totalitarianism, his warning would lose its force. His reader could remain complacent, detached from the urgent need for personal involvement in political change so emphasized by the animal allegory. If he had designed a political solution for the other beasts, furthermore, he could be accused of hypocrisy: his whole argument both inside and outside the text rested on the proposition that the people had to make and retain control of the revolution themselves if they wanted it to remain true to its goals. The deceit of the pigs was not the only failure on *Animal Farm*, for the foolish simplicity of the other animals and, indeed, of Old Major's naive idea of revolutionary change were as much to blame for the dictatorship which ensued. Orwell had to warn his readers that their apathy and thoughtlessness were as dangerous as blind admiration for the Stalinist regime. Only when all members of society saw the essential need for individual responsibility and honesty at the heart of any struggle for freedom and equality could the basic goals of Socialism, as Orwell saw them, be approached more closely. Meanwhile, no single revolutionary act could create a perfect world, either for the animals or for the humans whom they represent in the story. Acceptance of the notion of class struggle could not lead to an instant transformation of society unless those who would transform it accepted also the difficult burden of political power, both at the time of and after the revolution. While the most corrupting force on *Animal Farm* was the deception practiced upon the other animals by the pigs, the greatest danger came from the reluctance of the oppressed creatures to believe in an alternative between porcine and human rule. Yet it was in the affirmation of dignity, freedom, and equality tacitly provided by the nobler qualities of the presumed lower animals that Orwell saw the beginnings of such an alternative. So it is that, in the last moment of the book, he leaves open the task of rebuilding the revolution on a wiser and more cautiously optimistic foundation.

MICHAEL PETERS

'Animal Farm' *Fifty Years On*

Few books are as well-known as *Animal Farm*. Published fifty years ago, in August 1945, as the Cold War was about to begin, the novel with its mixture of simple fairy-tale and historical allegory, still has the power to charm and provoke, even though that war now seems to be part of a previous age. The novel, while frequently taught in schools to thirteen and fourteen year olds, is rarely to be found in sixth form or university syllabuses. Like the author, the book occupies an ambiguous place in the literary world. Yet its fame amongst the reading and, to an extent, the non-reading public is indisputable; the slogan, 'All animals are equal, but some are more equal than others', is one that has become part of the language.

Orwell was very clear about his intentions in writing the book. During the Spanish Civil War, he had seen the effects of the repressions and deceptions of Stalinism at first hand. He wished to open people's eyes to the reality of the Soviet regime 'in a story that could be easily understood by almost anyone', even when that regime had become an ally to Britain and the USA in the fight against German fascism. Such an exposure was essential, Orwell believed, if a true and democratic form of socialism was to be created. Working in London, first as a BBC journalist, and then as the literary editor of *Tribune*, *Animal Farm* was written whilst the bombs dropped; one bomb even damaged the manuscript when it fell on the street

From *Contemporary Review* 267:1555 (August 1995) 90–91. © 1995 by *Contemporary Review*.

where Orwell and his wife lived. Certainly the process by which the book saw the light of day was a tortuous one, with publisher after publisher finding reasons for refusing or delaying publication. For Gollancz, who had first option, and Faber, in the person of T. S. Eliot, the novel was too much of an attack on Russia, which had suffered so hugely at Stalingrad. Cape first consulted the Ministry of Information, who were concerned that the Russian leaders would take offence at their depiction as pigs, before turning the book down.

At the other end of the spectrum, even the Anarchist, Freedom Press, took exception to the novel. In America, the Dial Press thought it 'impossible to sell animal stories'. When, eventually, Warburg agreed to take the book, publication was delayed for almost a year, until the end of the European War. The question of whether this was due to a shortage of paper—the official explanation—or to political necessity, is still unresolved. From Paris, to which he travelled in February 1945, to report the War for *The Observer* at closer quarters, Orwell checked the proofs, making one last change. When the Windmill is attacked Napoleon stays standing, instead of dropping to the ground, as a tribute to Stalin's courage in remaining in Moscow during Hitler's advance; even to his enemies Orwell is determined to be fair.

Inevitably *Animal Farm*, when it was finally published, created controversy, although not of the kind originally envisaged. With the end of the struggle against fascism, a new conflict had begun to develop—the Cold War. Once effectively banned because of its politics, the book started to become an instrument of propaganda in the West's campaign to claim the moral high ground. Many new translations were produced, some with the assistance of the US State Department, and were circulated in places where Soviet influence prevailed—for example, the Ukraine and Korea. In 1947 the 'Voice of America' broadcast a radio version to Eastern Europe. The success of the novel in propaganda terms may be gauged by the Soviets' fear and loathing of the book, expressed by the seizure of copies in Germany, as well as by the cancellation of proposed radio dramatisations in Czechoslovakia. This occurred just before Soviet crackdowns in 1948 and again in 1968 on regimes which seemed to be dangerously libertarian.

Whilst Orwell was happy to see his book used to attack the Soviet myth, he did become increasingly worried about the way it was being used by the Right as a means of demonstrating that all revolutionary change was bound to fail. Picking out as central the moment when the pigs keep apples and milk for themselves, he makes the point that if 'the other animals had had the sense to put their foot down then it would have been all right'. Major's dream could have been realised. The masses should be 'alert', ready to 'chuck out their leaders as soon as they have done their job'. This is rather a different message than that found in the anti-Communist propaganda which so frequently surrounded, and surrounds, the novel.

For Orwell personally, *Animal Farm* marked his entry into the halls of literary fame. With the first impression of 4,500 copies soon sold out, sales in the UK reached 25,000 within five years, and over half a million in the US within four years. From being a marginal left-wing figure, Orwell became one of the most celebrated writers of the day, with periodic radio and television adaptations of both *Animal Farm* and *Nineteen Eighty Four*. In 1954, the first animated version of a literary text—a cartoon of *Animal Farm*—was made. However, in the last few years of his life, with a newly adopted son to bring up alone after his wife's unexpected death, and with his tuberculosis becoming increasingly serious, the success of what Orwell called his 'little squib' may have been some small comfort.

George Orwell, as many readers have done, recognised that the book's great achievement was to 'fuse political purpose and artistic purpose into one whole'. For this reason, fifty years on, in spite of the collapse of the Soviet system, in spite of the dilution of democratic socialism into liberalism, and in spite of the habit of literary critics to favour complex texts for deconstruction, *Animal Farm* may still be read with pleasure and profit, inside and outside the classroom, as one of the most imaginatively compelling satires on what Orwell called, in another of his fine phrases, the 'gramophone mind'.

Chronology

1903	George Orwell born Eric Arthur Blair, June 25th, at Motihari, Bengal, India. He is the only son of Richard Walmesley Blair, a subdeputy agent in the Opium Department of the Indian Civil Service, and Ida Mabel Limouzin. A sister, Marjorie Francis Blair, was born April 21, 1898.
1904	Returns to England with his mother and Marjorie.
1908	Attends Anglican day-school. A sister, Avril Nora, is born on April 6.
1911	Enters St. Cyprian's preparatory school.
1914	Publishes a patriotic poem, "Awake! Young Men of England," in *Henley and South Thames Oxfordshire Standard*.
1916	Graduates from St. Cyprian's.
1917	Enters Wellington College as a scholar; then Eton, where he is a member of the intellectually elite King's Scholars. Short stories and satirical poems published in *Election Times* and *College Days*.
1921	Leaves Eton with low academic standing.
1922	Joins the Imperial Indian Police; assistant superintendent of police at Rangoon, Burma.

1927	Returns to England and resigns from Imperial Service. Lives for awhile as a tramp to examine the conditions of the poor and exploited.
1928	Travels to Paris to become a writer. Contracts pneumonia and enters a Paris hospital. Publishes first journalistic work, "La Censure en Angleterre," in the French newspaper *Monde*, and "A Farthing Newspaper," in the English periodical *G.K.'s Weekly*.
1929	Returns to England.
1930	Writes book reviews for *New Adelphi*.
1932	Considers several pen names, including "George Orwell," but continues to write as Eric Blair until December 1936. Teaches at The Hawthornes, a private school for boys age 10 to 16.
1933	*Down and Out in Paris and London* published. Teaches at Frays College, Middlesex; becomes ill and enters Uxbridge hospital in November with pneumonia.
1934	His first novel, *Burmese Days*, published in the United States; moves to London and works as part-time assistant at Booklovers' Corner, Hampstead.
1935	His second novel, *A Clergyman's Daughter*, and *Burmese Days* published in England; articles and reviews published in the *New English Weekly*.
1936	*Keep the Aspidistra Flying* published. Marries Eileen O'Shaughnessy; travels to Barcelona, Spain.
1937	*The Road to Wigan Pier* published by the Left Book Club. Fights in the Spanish Civil War and is wounded in the throat by a Fascist sniper. Escapes with Eileen into France; returns to England.
1938	*Homage to Catalonia* published. Joins Independent Labor Party. Enters a sanitarium for six months after suffering a tubercular lesion in one lung. Travels with Eileen to Morocco.

1939   *Coming Up for Air* published. Returns to England; tries to enlist in Army but is rejected because of tuberculosis. Father dies of cancer on June 28.

1940   *Inside the Whale*, a collection of essays, published. Moves to London and joins Home Guard Batallion.

1941   *The Lion and the Unicorn: Socialism and the English Genius* published; two essays appear in *The Betrayal of the Left*. First "London Letters" articles published in *Partisan Review*. Joins Indian bureau of the BBC Far Eastern Service.

1943   Mother dies March 19. Leaves Home Guard because of poor health; resigns from BBC; becomes literary editor of the *Tribune*; reviews books for the *Manchester Evening News*.

1944   *Animal Farm* rejected by several publishers before being accepted by Secker & Warburg. The Blairs adopt an infant boy and christen him Richard Horatio Blair.

1945   *Animal Farm* published. War correspondent in France, Germany, and Austria for *The Observer* and *The Manchester Evening News*. Eileen dies during surgery.

1946   *Critical Essays* published in England, in America as *Dickens, Dali and Others*. Marjorie Blair (Dakin) dies May 3.

1947   Becomes ill with tuberculosis of left lung; enters Hairmyres Hospital near Glasgow, Scotland. Completes first draft of *Nineteen Eighty-Four*.

1948   First volume of Secker & Warburg Uniform Edition of writings published. Returns from hospital; completes *Nineteen Eighty-Four*.

1949   *Nineteen Eighty-Four* published. Enters Cotswold Sanitarium, then University College Hospital in London. Marries Sonia Brownell.

1950   Dies of pulmonary tuberculosis on January 21; buried, as Eric Arthur Blair, at Sutton Courtenay churchyard, Berkshire.

Contributors

HAROLD BLOOM is Sterling Professor of Humanities at Yale University and Professor of English at New York University. His works include *Shelley's Mythmaking* (1959), *The Visionary Company* (1961), *The Anxiety of Influence* (1973), *Agon: Towards a Theory of Revisionism* (1982), *The Book of J* (1990), *The American Religion* (1992), and *The Western Canon* (1994). His forthcoming books are a study of Shakespeare and *Freud, Transference and Authority*, which considers all of Freud's major writings. A MacArthur Prize Fellow, Professor Bloom is the editor of more than thirty anthologies and general editor of five series of literary criticism published by Chelsea House.

NORTHROP FRYE (1912–1991) was Professor Emeritus at the University of Toronto, and one of the major literary critics in the Western tradition. Among his many published works are *Fearful Symmetry* (1947), *Anatomy of Criticism* (1957), and *The Great Code: The Bible and Literature* (1982).

ROBERT A. LEE is the author of several works of literary criticism, including *Orwell's Fiction* (1969), *Alistair MacLean: The Key is Fear* (1976), and *James Baldwin: Climbing to the Light* (1991).

RICHARD I. SMYER is Associate Professor of English at the University of Arizona, Tucson, where he teaches political fiction, the short story, British Commonwealth literature, and detective fiction. His published works include *Primal Dream and Primal Crime: Orwell's Development as a Psychological Novelist* (1979) and articles on V.S. Naipaul, Nadine Gordimer, and P.D. James.

BERNARD CRICK is Emeritus Professor of Politics at Birkbeck College, the University of London. He has written many articles and several books, including *George Orwell: A Life* (1980) and *Orwell and the Business of Biography* (1996).

DAPHNE PATAI is the author of *Forms of Myth in Contemporary Brazilian Fiction* (1977); editor, with Angela Ingram, of *Rediscovering Forgotten Radicals: British Women Writers 1889–1939* (1993) and editor, with Noretta Koertge, of *Professing Feminism: Cautionary Tales from the Strange World of Women's Studies* (1994).

PATRICK REILLY is the author of many books, including *Jonathan Swift: The Brave Desponder* (1982), *Nineteen Eighty-Four: Past, Present, and Future* (1989), and *Lord of the Flies: Fathers and Sons* (1992).

ROBERT SOLOMON is Associate Professor of Philosophy at the University of Texas, Austin. His published works include many books on nineteenth and twentieth-century philosophy and two books on the philosophy of the emotions, *The Passions: Emotions and the Meaning of Life* (1993) and *The Philosophy of Love* (1991).

LARAINE FERGENSON is the author of *Wordsworth and Thoreau; A Study of the Relationship Between Man and Nature* (1971) and *The American Response to British Romanticism* (1987).

V.C. LETEMENDIA is an Adjunct Professor in the Department of Political Science, University of Toronto. Her field of interest is the relationship between politics and literature. Forthcoming is a comparative study of the political ideas of George Orwell and Albert Camus.

MICHAEL PETERS is the editor of *Education and the Postmodern Condition*, with foreword by Jean-Francois Lyotard (1995), and author of *Poststructuralism, Politics, and Education* (1996).

Bibliography

Carter, Thomas. "Group Psychology Phenomena of a Political System as Satirized in *Animal Farm:* An Application of the Theories of W.R. Bion." *Human Relations* 27 (1974): 525–46.

Cooper, Nancy M. "*Animal Farm:* An Explication for Teachers of Orwell's Novel." *California English Journal* 4 (1968): 59–69.

Davis, Robert M. "Politics in the Pig-Pen." *Journal of Popular Culture* 2 (1968): 314-20.

Eliot, T.S. "T.S. Eliot and *Animal Farm*: Reasons for Rejection." *Times* London (January 6, 1969): 9

Greenblatt, Stephen Jay. *Three Modern Satirists: Waugh, Orwell, and Huxley.* New Haven: Yale University Press, 1965. 65.

Hoggart, Richard. "Walking the Tight Rope: *Animal Farm.*" *Speaking to Each Other,* Volume 2. New York: Oxford University Press; London: Chatto and Windus, 1970. 108–10.

Kressel, Marilyn. "Pigs on Two Feet: George Orwell Through the Prism of Watergate." *Intellect* 103 (1974): 192–95.

Lee, Robert A. "The Uses of Form: A Reading of *Animal Farm.*" *Studies in Short Fiction* 6 (1969): 557–73.

Meyers, Jeffrey. "Orwell's Bestiary: The Political Allegory of *Animal Farm.*" *Studies in the Twentieth Century* 8 (1971): 65–84.

———, ed. *George Orwell: the Critical Heritage.* Boston: Routledge & Kegan Paul Ltd., 1975. 195–208.

Warburg, Fredric. "*Animal Farm* and *1984.*" *All Authors Are Equal.* London: Hutchinson, 1973. New York: St. Martin's Press, 1974. 8–15, 35–58, 92–120, 205–06.

Acknowledgments

"Orwell and Marxism" by Northrop Frye from *Northrop Frye: On Culture and Literature: A Collection of Review Essays*, edited by Robert D. Denham. Copyright © 1978 by Northrop Frye. This essay originally appeared in *The Canadian Forum* 26 (December 1946). Reprinted by permission.

"Animal Farm" by Robert A. Lee from *Orwell's Fiction*, by Robert A. Lee. Copyright © 1969 by University of Notre Dame Press. Reprinted by permission.

"*Animal Farm*: The Burden of Consciousness" by Richard I. Smyer from *English Language Notes* 9:1 (September 1971). Copyright © 1971 by the Regents of the University of Colorado, Boulder. Reprinted by permission.

"The Making of *Animal Farm*" by Bernard Crick from *George Orwell: A Life* by Bernard Crick, © 1980 by Bernard Crick. Reprinted in *Critical Essays on George Orwell*, edited by Bernard Oldsey and Joseph Browne. Copyright © 1986 by Bernard Oldsey and Joseph Browne. Reprinted by permission.

"Political Fiction and Patriarchal Fantasy" by Daphne Patai from *The Orwell Mystique: A Study in Male Ideology* by Daphne Patai. Copyright © 1984 by Daphne Patai. Reprinted by permission.

"The Utopian Shipwreck" by Patrick Reilly from *George Orwell: The Age's Adversary* by Patrick Reilly. Copyright ©1986 by Patrick Reilly. Reprinted by permission.

"Ant Farm: An Orwellian Allegory" by Robert Solomon from *Reflections on America, 1984: An Orwell Symposium*, edited by Robert Mulvihill. Copyright © 1986 by the University of Georgia Press. Reprinted by permission.

143

Index

All Authors Are Equal (Warburg), 41
Allies, warring parties as, 10
"*Animal Farm*" (Lee), 7–24
Animal Farm, 10, 13, 113, 117
  as anatomy of all political revolutions,
    10
  ant farm as allegory for, 91–107
  as beast fable, 1, 8–9, 11, 47–48,
    61–62, 64, 109–18
  children's literature and, 1–2, 48
  corruption of language in, 7–24
  critical reception of, 9–10, 111–12
  as feminist fable, 58–60
  Gulliver's Travel's and, 62–89
  honesty in, 7–24, 85
  joy in, 64–70
  making of, 29–43
  origin and purpose of, 30, 46,
    109–10, 119–29, 131–32
  as patriarchal fantasy, 45–60
  publishing of, 31–42, 47, 64, 111,
    121–22, 132
  as satire on current higher education,
    2
  success of, 131–33
  unused prefaces of, 42–43, 111,
    119–29
"*Animal Farm*: The Burden of
  Consciousness" (Smyer), 25–28
"'*Animal Farm*' Fifty Years On"
  (Peters), 131–33
Animals
  equality of, 3, 22–23, 25, 117

gender dividing, 45–60
inability of to recognize oppression,
  17–21
mental incapacity of and lack of
  consciousness of evil, 25–28
"Ant Farm: An Orwellian Allegory"
  (Solomon), 91–107
Ant farm, as allegory for *Animal Farm*,
  91–107
Arendt, Hannah, 92
Aristotle, 89
"Arthur Koestler" (Orwell), 7, 62
"Art of Donald McGill, The" (Orwell),
  7
Astor, David, 40
Austen, Jane, 76

Barber, Frank, 42
Beast fable
  Animal Farm as, 1, 8–9, 11, 47–48,
    61–62, 64, 109–18
  psychological appeal of, 47–48
Beasts of England, 19, 48, 51, 82
Benjamin, 1, 23
  change and, 23
  cynicism of, 11
  friendship between Boxer and, 57
  intelligence of, 21–22, 23, 25, 27–28,
    71–72, 76–77, 116–17, 118
  Orwell versus, 81–82
  reading and, 80
Berneri, Marie Louise, 40

Bloom, Harold, 1–2
Boxer, 1, 18, 19, 20–21, 22, 25, 58, 65,
  66, 76, 77
  anthropomorphic terms used for, 45
  credulity of, 78–79
  death of, 117
  exploitation of, 77, 78–79
  faith of in Napoleon, 21, 23, 78, 84,
    114
  as fool, 70
  friendship between Benjamin and, 57
  as knacker, 75–76
  reaction to carnage of, 69
  reading and, 80, 116
  solicitude of, 65
  stupidity of, 20–21, 23, 70–71, 72,
    114
  as worker, 1, 4, 49, 51
Buddicom, Jacintha, 41
Burckhardt, 68
Burdekin, Katharine, 48–49
Burmese Days (Orwell), 8, 17, 24, 64

Cape, Jonathan, 34–36, 37, 42, 111,
  121–22, 132
Capitalism, *Animal Farm* attacking, 86
Card game, Teheran Conference as, 10
Cat
  good intentions of, 15
  re-education of, 78
  selfishness of, 72, 77
  work avoided by, 51
Chaucer, Geoffrey, 1, 84
Children's literature, *Animal Farm* and,
  1–2, 48
Church, Moses as, 58
Churchill, Winston, 31, 50, 79
Clergyman's Daughter, A (Orwell), 17
Clifford, Gay, 47
Clover, 1, 11, 15, 19, 23, 25, 56–57
  awareness of, 21
  Boxer ignoring warnings of, 79
  inarticulateness of, 23
  as maternal, 49–51, 57–58, 67
  reaction of to carnage, 69

weakness of, 21
Cold War, *Animal Farm* and, 132–33
Comfort, Alex, 50
Coming Up For Air (Orwell), 7, 8, 50
Communism. *See* Russian Communism
Confession, dramatization of spurious,
  17–18
Cooper, Lettice, 31
Cowshed, Battle of the, 18, 78, 80
Crick, Bernard, 29, 111, 125

Dante Called You Beatrice (Potts), 41
Darkness at Noon (Kingsley), 18, 74
Deutsch, Andre, 121
Dial Press, 40, 47, 132
Dickens, Charles, 2, 82
Down and Out in Paris and London
  (Orwell), 39
Dyson, A. E., 10

"Earth's Holocaust" (Hawthorne), 73
Eliot, T.S., 36–39, 42, 62, 64, 71, 79,
  111, 122, 126, 132
Empson, William, 88, 114, 117
Engels, Friedrich, 4
England
  Orwell on family in, 59
  Orwell urging population policies for,
    55–56
  reception of *Animal Farm* in, 111
"English People, The" (Orwell), 55–56
Equality
  of animals, 3, 22–23, 25, 117
  perversion of, 14–15
Ethics, ant farm allegory and, 95–107
Evil
  corruption of language and inability
    to ascertain truth and, 7–24
  expunged with removal of one single
    enemy, 72–76
  intelligence and, 14–15, 61, 70–72,
    79–80, 114–15, 118
  mental incapacity of animals and lack
    of consciousness of, 25–28

Exploitation, end of, 79, 80–81

Faber & Faber, 37–39, 42, 111, 122, 132
Falsification, 16–21
  corruption of language and inability
    to ascertain truth and, 7–24
Family, Orwell on, 59
Female reproductive labor, 55
  as part of society's productive activi-
    ties, 53–57
  state expropriation of, 55
Feminist interpretation, *Animal Farm*
  as patriarchal fantasy as, 45–60
Fergenson, Laraine, 109–18
Frederick, 16, 20, 110
  as Germany, 10
"Freedom of the Press, The" (Orwell),
  111
Freedom Press, 40, 132
Friendship, male, 57
Frye, Northrop, 3–5, 47

Gender hierarchy, *Animal Farm* repro-
  ducing, 45–60
George, Daniel, 34, 35
"George Orwell's *Animal Farm*: A
  Twentieth-Century Beast Fable"
  (Fergenson), 109–18
Germany, warring parties as, 10
"Gerontion" (Eliot), 71
Gide, André, 63
Gladiators, The (Koestler), 62
Goldstein, Emmanuel, 12
Gollancz, Victor, 31–34, 35, 39, 40,
  111, 121, 132
Gorer, Geoffrey, 125
Grahame, Kenneth, 1
Gulliver's Travels (Swift), 1, 39, 62–89

Hammond, J. R., 115
"Hanging, A" (Orwell), 9
Hawthorne, Nathaniel, 73
Heppenstall, Rayner, 83

Hitler, Adolf, 31, 63, 71, 79, 110
Hollis, Christopher, 8
Homage to Catalonia (Orwell), 62, 64,
  70, 78
Honesty, in *Animal Farm*, 7–25, 85
Hopkinson, Tom, 8, 9–10
Howe, Irving, 12
Human beings, Orwell's opposition to,
  81–84

Ibsen, Henrik, 71
"Inside the Whale" (Orwell), 7, 50, 60,
  116
Instinct, political absolutism versus, 15
Intelligence
  of Benjamin, 21–22, 23, 25, 27–28,
    61, 70–72, 76–77, 116–17, 118
  evil and, 14–15, 25–28, 61, 70–72,
    79–80, 114–15, 118
  exploitation and, 57
  of Napoleon, 115
  of pigs, 7–24, 26–27, 57, 79–80, 87
  of Snowball, 115

Jones, Farmer, 14, 27, 79
  action controlled by, 20
  animals resembling, 3, 52, 53, 57, 73,
    75
  death, 64–65
  as "Everyman," 10
  exploitation and, 81
  irresponsibility of, 11, 12, 72, 73
  ouster of, 13, 27, 52, 80
  pigs or Jones as leader as option, 79,
    127, 128
  Snowball and, 78
Joy, in *Animal Farm*, 64–70
Joyce, James, 63
Just society, 62, 84
  Major's speech and, 11–12, 19, 53–54,
    70, 72–76, 79, 124–25

Karl, Frederick, 9

Keats, John, 72
Keep the Aspidistra Flying (Orwell), 22
Koestler, Arthur, 4, 17, 62, 79

Language, corruption of, 7–24
Laski, Harold, 42
Lawrence, D. H., 86
Lee, Robert A., 7–24
Lenin, V. I., 34
  Major as, 10
  Napoleon as, 110
Letemendia, V. C., 119–29
*Lion and the Unicorn: Socialism and the
  English Genius, The* (Orwell), 7,
  59
"Looking Back on the Spanish War"
  (Orwell), 7, 116

Macdonald, Dwight, 42, 120, 125–26,
  127, 128
MacIntyre, Alasdair, 93
Major, 1, 14, 20, 52, 57, 80, 85, 128
  female labor and, 53–54
  as Lenin, 10
  orthodoxy and, 88
  as patriarch, 49
  Seven Commandments and, 59
  speech of, 11–12, 19, 53–54, 70,
    72–76, 79, 124–25
"Making of *Animal Farm*, The"
  (Crick), 29–43
Mann, Thomas, 68, 81
Mansfield Park (Austen), 76
Marcuse, Herbert, 67
Mario and the Magician (Mann), 81
"Marrakech" (Orwell), 45–46
Marx, Karl, 4, 34, 71
Marxism. *See* Russian Communism
Maternal imagery, in *Animal Farm*,
  49–51, 57–58, 67
Mental incapacity, animals' lack of
  consciousness of evil and, 25–26
Mollie, 57
  defection of, 67

as heretic, 15
as human female, 51
patriarchy understood by, 58
reading and, 80
selfish folly of, 72
vanity of, 11, 15
work avoided by, 51
Moore, 35, 39, 41–42
Moses, 62
  as church, 58
  religious satire and, 17

Napoleon, 12, 14, 19, 20, 58, 74, 76
  accomplishments of, 13
  as ambitious, 5
  Boxer's faith in, 21, 23, 78, 84, 114
  Boxer's remains and, 117
  Boxer versus, 66
  Clover and, 51
  as comic cheat, 66
  exploitation and, 79
  falsification and windmill construc-
    tion and, 16–17
  father role of, 52
  hate for, 64
  human resemblance of, 3, 22–23
  individuality and, 2
  intelligence of, 115
  leadership of, 126, 127
  as Lenin and Stalin, 1, 10, 18, 88, 110
  as Moloch, 69
  as patriarch, 49, 52–53
  Snowball as scapegoat and, 17–18
  Snowball versus, 52, 80, 110, 112
  as society's martyr, 81
  Swift and, 68
  trade with outside world and, 27
  as wrong, 84
New Economic Policy, windmill as,
  16
Nietzsche, 69, 75
Nineteen Eighty-Four (Orwell), 1, 12,
  18, 21, 24, 29, 30, 47, 56, 57, 60,
  63, 65, 66, 68, 71, 88–89, 91, 92,
  93, 113, 116, 122, 133

"Orwell and Marxism" (Frye), 3–5
Orwell, George
  "Arthur Koestler," 7, 62
  "The Art of Donald McGill," 7
  Burmese Days, 8, 17, 24, 64
  A Clergyman's Daughter, 17
  Coming Up For Air, 7, 8, 50
  Down and Out in Paris and London, 39
  "The English People," 55–56
  "The Freedom of the Press," 111
  "A Hanging," 9
  Homage to Catalonia, 62, 64, 70, 78
  "Inside the Whale," 7, 50, 60, 116
  Keep the Aspidistra Flying, 22
  The Lion and the Unicorn, 7, 59
  "Looking Back on the Spanish War,"
    7, 116
  "Marrakech," 45–46
  Nineteen Eighty-Four, 1, 12, 18, 21,
    24, 29, 30, 47, 56, 57, 60, 63, 65,
    66, 68, 71, 88–89, 91, 92, 93, 113,
    116, 122, 133
  relief of human suffering as priority
    of, 63
  The Road to Wigan Pier, 117
  "Shooting an Elephant," 9
  on success of *Animal Farm*, 131–33
  Swift and, 62–89
  "Why I Write," 8, 109
  See also Animal Farm

Patai, Daphne, 45–60
Patriarchal fantasy, *Animal Farm* as,
  45–60
Paul, St., 71
Pessimism, failure of revolutions and,
  25–28
Peters, Michael, 131–33
Phillips, William, 125
Pigs
  absurdity of, 121
  as boars, 49
  deception of, 128, 129
  exploitation and, 80–81
  intelligence of, 26–27, 57, 79–80, 87

language controlled by, 7–24
patriarchy established by, 52–58
pigs or Jones as leader as option, 79,
  127, 128
reading and, 80–81
softness of, 57
Pilkington, 16, 20, 85, 86
  as Allies, 10
Plato, 81
Plowman, Dorothy, 31
"Political Fiction and Patriarchal
  Fantasy" (Patai), 45–60
Population policies, Orwell on, 55–56
Potts, Paul, 40–41
Pound, Ezra, 63
Power
  intentions corrupted by, 23
  righteousness and, 61, 70, 76
Protective gesture, Clover and, 50–51
Proud Man (Burdekin), 48–49

Rahv, Philip, 29, 125
Read, Herbert, 42
Reading, 115–16
  character defined by, 80–81
Reality, corruption of language and
  lack of recognition of, 7–24
Rees, Richard, Sir, 10
Reilly, Patrick, 61–89
Religious satire, *Animal Farm* as, 17,
  23
Revolution
  corruption of, 7–24
  failure of, 26–27, 50–51, 77–78,
    85–86, 87–89
  individual responsibility for, 119–29
  patriarchy reestablished by, 52–58
"Revolution on Animal Farm: Orwell's
  Neglected Commentary" (Lete-
  mendia), 119–29
Rhondda, Lady, 36, 122
Richards, I. A., 9
Richards, Vernon, 40
Ridenour, Louis, 111–12, 114
Righteousness, power and, 61, 70, 76

Road to Wigan Pier, The (Orwell), 117

Russell, Bertrand, 127

Russian Communism, *Animal Farm* as satire on, 1, 2, 3–5, 10, 23, 31–34, 35, 42, 46, 48–49, 57, 86–87, 93, 113, 118, 123, 124, 126–27, 128, 132

Russian Revolution, 25, 30, 49, 110, 113, 127

Russo-German alliance, timber deal as, 10

Schiller, Johann, 68

Secker & Warburg, 39–40, 41–42, 111

Seven Commandments, 14, 17, 19–20, 28, 48, 59, 116, 117

Sexual politics, on farm, 52–58

"Shooting an Elephant" (Orwell), 9

Slater, Philip, 93

Smyer, Richard I., 25–28

Snowball, 2, 3–4, 12, 18, 22, 78, 84, 88

  accomplishments of, 13

  Battle of the Cowshed and, 80

  committees and, 115

  falsification and windmill constriction and, 16–17

  ferocity of, 65

  flight from Napoleon's dogs, 69

  intelligence of, 115

  Napoleon versus, 52, 80, 110, 112

  as scapegoat, 17–18

  as Trotsky, 1, 10, 110

  work encouraged by, 77

Solomon, Robert, 91–107

Soule, George, 112

Squealer, 12, 16, 19, 20, 22, 52, 78, 128

  just society and, 84

  on leadership of pigs, 81

  pigs' theft of the milk and apples and, 125

  trickery of, 64

Stalin, Joseph, 31–33, 34, 57, 67, 79, 83, 86, 87–88, 112, 118, 121, 123, 124, 127

  Napoleon as, 1, 10, 18, 88, 110

  Orwell attacking, 87

Struve, Gleb, 29

Swift, Jonathan, 1, 4, 39, 62–89

  Gulliver's Travels, 62–69

  The Tale of the Tub, 4, 68, 87

Tale of the Tub, The (Swift), 4, 68, 87

Teheran Conference, 30, 123

  card game as, 10

Theory and Practice of Oligarchical Collectivism, The (Goldstein), 12

Timber deal, as Russo-German alliance, 10

Tolstoy, Leo, 63

Totalitarianism, individual values protecting against

  See also Russian Communism

Trotsky, Leon, 34, 88, 112–13

  Snowball as, 1, 10, 110

United States, reception of *Animal Farm* in, 47, 111

Utopia, Orwell against, 72–76

"Utopian Shipwreck, The" (Reilly), 61–89

Voltaire, 91, 92

Wain, John, 8–9

Warburg, Frederick, 40, 41–42, 122, 132

Wedgwood, Veronica, 34, 35, 36

Weinbaum, Batya, 52, 58

White, E. B., 92

Whitman Press, 41

"Why I Write" (Orwell), 8, 109

Wind in the Willows, The (Grahame), 1

Windmill
  Battle of the, 110
  rebuilding of, 83
  as secular heaven, 16–17, 19, 20
  treachery destroying, 74
Woodcock, George, 40

Woodhouse, C. M., 113
World War II, 20, 25, 110

Ziolkowski, Jan, 113

Hopkinsville-Christian County Public Library
1101 BETHEL STREET
HOPKINSVILLE, KENTUCKY 42240